Alice Lucas

Translations from the German Poets of the 18th and 19th Centuries

Alice Lucas

Translations from the German Poets of the 18th and 19th Centuries

ISBN/EAN: 9783337189570

Printed in Europe, USA, Canada, Australia, Japan

Cover: Foto ©Thomas Meinert / pixelio.de

More available books at **www.hansebooks.com**

EIN GLEICHNISZ.

Jüngst pflückt ich einen Wiesenstrauss
Trug ihn gedankenvoll nach Haus;
Da hatten von der warmen Hand,
Die Kronen sich alle zur Erde-gewandt
Ich setzt sie in ein frisches Glas
Und welch ein Wünder war mir das!
Die Köpfchen hoben sich empor,
Die Blätterstengel ine grünen Flor
Und allzusammen so gesund,
Als ständen sie noch auf Muttergrund.

So war mir's, als ich wundersam,
Mein Lied in fremder Sprache vernahm.
Goethe.

TRANSLATIONS

FROM

THE GERMAN POETS

OF THE 18TH AND 19TH CENTURIES

BY

ALICE LUCAS

HENRY S. KING & CO., LONDON
1876

PREFATORY NOTE.

IN the following Translations the principal object has been to preserve strict fidelity; the original metres have been, with very few exceptions, carefully preserved. Thus it is hoped that while those unacquainted with the originals may have some idea of them here presented, German scholars will find their old favourites in a garb not wholly unsuited to them.

A few Poems are by another hand than that of the Translator of the main portion of them. These are distinguished by initials.

CONTENTS.

PAGE

JOHANN GEORG JACOBI. [1740-1814.]
LITANY ON ALL SOULS' DAY, ... 1

JOHANN G. von HERDER. [1744-1803.]
NIGHT. A FRAGMENT, ... 5
THE LYRE, ... 8

MATTHIAS CLAUDIUS. [1740-1815.]
AN EVENING HYMN, ... 12
THE LOST STAR, ... 14
THE SPRING. ON THE FIRST MAY MORNING, . 16

LUDWIG H. C. HÖLTY. [1748-1776.]
SONG, ... 17

FRIEDRICH L. von STOLBERG. [1750-1819.]

	PAGE
THE MOUNTAIN TORRENT,	19

JOHANN WOLFGANG von GOETHE. [1749-1832.]

MIGNON,	22
THE FISHER,	23
— A WANDERER'S EVENING SONG,	25
ANOTHER,	26
DEDICATION,	27
THE VIOLET,	34
THE LOVED ONE NEAR,	35
THE MINSTREL,	37
— A HARPER'S SONG,	39
TO MIGNON,	40
THE WEDDING SONG,	42

FRIEDERICH von SCHILLER. [1759-1805.]

THE LAMENT OF CERES,	47
THE FISHER-BOY,	55
DESIRE,	56
THE FEAST OF VICTORY,	58
DITHYRAMBE,	68
THE GODS OF GREECE,	70
THE YOUTH AT THE BROOK,	79
THE COUNT OF HABSBURG,	81

SCHMIDT von LÜBECK. [1766-1849.]

THE STRANGER'S EVENING SONG,	89

CONTENTS.

FRIEDERICH von MATTHISSON. [1761-1831.]

	PAGE
ADELAIDE,	92
AN EVENING LANDSCAPE,	93

F. GAUDENZ von SALIS-SEEWIS. [1762-1834.]

PSYCHE'S GRIEF,	96

LUDWICK TIECK. [1773-1853.]

AUTUMN SONG,	99
NIGHT,	101

CLEMENS BRENTANO. [1777-1842.]

I SOUGHT TO BIND A POSY,	103
TO SEVILLA,	105

JOSEPH FREIHERR von EICHENDORF. [1788-1857.]

THE BROKEN RING,	107
ABROAD,	109
GRIEF,	110

ERNST MORITZ ARNDT. [1769-1860.]

THE SOLACE OF TEARS,	112

THEODOR KÖRNER. [1791-1813.]

THE DEATH-SONG,	114
TO SPRING,	115
PRAYER DURING BATTLE,	117

ADALBERT CHAMISSO DE BONCOURT.
[1781-1838.]

	PAGE
CASTLE BONCOURT,	119
THE LION BRIDE,	122

LUDWIG UHLAND. [1787-1862.]

THE MINSTREL'S CURSE,	126
THE HOSTESS' DAUGHTER,	133
FAITHFUL WALTER,	135
DREAM,	138
THE SERENADE,	139
THE SHEPHERD'S SABBATH SONG,	140
PARTING,	141

FRIEDERICH RÜCKERT. [1789-1866.]

BARBAROSSA,	144

JUSTINUS KERNER. [1786-1862.]

THE DYING MILLER,	147
TO THE DRINKING-GLASS OF A DEPARTED FRIEND,	148

WILHELM MÜLLER. [1795-1827.]

SONG,	150
VINETA,	151

CONTENTS. xi

HEINRICH HEINE. [1800-1856.]

PAGE
SONG, ... 154
THE LOTUS FLOWER, ... 156
SONG, ... 157
SONG, ... 157
SONG, ... 159
ANOTHER, ... 160
THE WATER-LILY, ... 161
THE LURELEI, ... 162
WE SAT IN A LITTLE BOAT, LOVE, . . . 164
I SEE THEE OFT IN DREAMS AGAIN, . . . 165
I DREAMED, ... 166
SONG, ... 167

HOFFMANN von FALLERSLEBEN. [1798-   .]

PARTING, ... 168
CRADLE SONG, ... 169

J. C. FREIHERR von ZEDLITZ. [1790-1862.]

THE ROBBER'S WIFE, ... 171

NICOLAUS LENAU. [1802-1850.]

THE GIPSIES, ... 174
SEDGE SONG, ... 176

ANNETTE von DROSTE HÜLFSHOF.
[1798-1848.]

	PAGE
THE MERCHANT'S WIFE,	178

ANASTASIUS GRÜN. [1806-   .]

MANHOOD'S TEAR,	184

ERNST von FEUCHTERSLEBEN. [1806-1849.]

IT IS ALMIGHTY GOD'S DECREE,	186

WILHELM WACKERNAGEL. [1806-1869.]

THE WEEPING WILLOW,	188

EMANUEL GEIBEL. [1815-   .]

FROM AFAR,	190
THE WANDERING SPANIARD,	192
MY HEART IS LIKE THE GLOOMY NIGHT,	195

GOTTFRIED KINKEL. [1815-   .]

EVENING HYMN,	196

TRANSLATIONS FROM THE WORKS OF GERMAN POETS.

JOHANN GEORG JACOBI.
[1740—1814.]

LITANY ON ALL SOULS' DAY.

Now in peace all souls repose;
They who passed through many woes,
They whose lot was bright as morn,
Sick of life, or newly born;
Now their earthly days they cease,
Now all spirits rest in peace.

They who sought companions e'er,
Often wept, yet murmured ne'er,
When the pressure of the hand
None they met would understand;
Now their earthly life they cease,
Now all spirits rest in peace.

Maidens' souls, whose loving woe
Caused unnumbered tears to flow,
Those whom faithless friends betray,
And the blind world casts away,
Now their earthly life they cease,
Now all spirits rest in peace.

And the youth, whose gentle bride,
Since it was for love he died,
Comes his grave at early morn
With a taper to adorn;

Now their earthly life they cease,

Now all spirits rest in peace.

All the spirits who, from youth,

Wore the martyr's crown of truth,

Striving for a holy aim,

Seeking not the martyr's fame,

Now their earthly life they cease,

Now all spirits rest in peace.

Those who ne'er beheld the noon,

But on thorns, beneath the moon

Watched until the time when they

Greet the Lord's eternal day;

Now their earthly life they cease,

Now all spirits rest in peace.

Those who 'midst the roses fair,

Loved the sparkling wine to share,

But in times of sore distress
Tasted all its bitterness;
Now their earthly life they cease,
Now all spirits rest in peace.

Those who knew no peace or rest,
But whose strength and faith were blest,
On the field with corpses strewn,
In the sleeping world alone;
Now their earthly life they cease,
Now all spirits rest in peace.

Now in peace all souls repose;
They who passed through many woes,
They whose lot was bright as morn,
Sick of life, or newly born;
Now their earthly days they cease,
Now all spirits rest in peace.

JOHANN G. VON HERDER.
[1744—1803.]

NIGHT. A FRAGMENT.

ART returning, peaceful holy mother
Of the stars and heavenly meditation—
Art to us returning? Earth is waiting
Yearningly for thee, and all her flowers
Bend their weary heads, from out thy chalice
Fragrant drops of heaven's dew desiring.
And with them inclineth too my weary
Soul, with wondrous images o'ercrowded,
Waiting till the gentle hand efface them—
Images of other worlds' creating,
And with rest my yearning heart refresheth.

Star-bespangled, golden-crownéd goddess,
Thou upon whose sable garments flowing
Sparkle tens of thousands worlds, whom gently
Thou hast borne, and whose unceasing motion,
Fiery orbits' course, and restless being,
Thou with arms of rest eternal holdest.
With what hymns of praise to thee resoundeth
All the universe, thou gentle leader
Of the starry chorus, hymns, and praises,
Silencing the tempest, softly lulling
Into slumber every voice and language,
Ev'ry whisp'ring heart in holy silence !
Holy silence, now the world o'erbrooding,
Gentle stream, that on the shores eternal
Of the vast creation rolleth ever ;
And thou music of those worlds celestial,
Light from light, the heavens' gentle language !

· · · · ·

Lofty night, I kneel before thy altar;

All the lights in th' all-surrounding ether

Are the fillet of thy holy temples,

Full of sacred letters. Who can read them,

Flaming letters of the Uncreated

On the brow of night? They say: Jehovah

Is the only God, His name Eternal,

And His child is Night; her name is calléd

Mystery: no mortal e'er hath lifted

Yet her veil most holy. She created

Worlds, and space, and time. Her children ever

Stand in face of love, and law, and order,

And of fate relentless, guiding ever—

Guiding ever to the loving Father.

Fling around thy veil, O holy mother!

Close thy mighty book of sacred writing!

Even in my thoughts I can no higher,

Can no further climb; do thou then rather

Pour from out thy sleep-filled horn upon me,
Gently pour on me, O holy mother
Thou of sleep and dreams, pour gently on me
Soft oblivion of my cares and sorrows.

THE LYRE.

Ye chords, what singeth in you?
What sounds do ye prolong?
Is't thou, oh Philomela,
Thou bird of mournful song?
Who when she to my spirit
Her soft complaining sent,
Became, perchance, in sighing,
A silver instrument.

Ye chords, what speaketh in you?
What sounds do ye prolong?

Dost thou, oh love, deceive me
With echo's sweetest song?
Thou who all hearts beguilest,
All lips in love that meet,
Art thou in tones imprisoned,
Perchance, oh nymph! most fleet?

The voice grows louder, stronger,
And to my heart draws nigh,
And wakes with touch enchanted
The grief of years gone by.
O soul! thou tremblest in me,
Thyself a lyre art grown;
What spirit is't that holds thee
With feeling's quivering tone?

Throughout the chords it gloweth,
It whispers in my ear,

The universal spirit
Of harmony is near.
'Tis I, who ev'ry creature
To shape and form compel,
And pierce their inmost nature
With sympathetic spell.

In dark and flinty caverns
I am the echo strong;
I thrill, with softer cadence,
In Philomela's low song.
In sad laments I fill thee
With pity's tender pain,
And raise thy heart to heaven
In holy, prayerful strain.

'Tis I attune creation
To one mysterious note,

An everlasting chorus,

Where soul to soul doth float.

Through all thy heart a trembling,

By music wakened, steals,

And sorrow's gentle gladness,

And joy's sweet grief it feels.

Be hushed, O voice! I hearken,

Creation's chorus vast,

That heart to heart, and spirit

To spirit bindeth fast.

We, in one great emotion,

Are an eternal whole,

One tone where all are mingled,

The Godhead's echoed soul.

MATTHIAS CLAUDIUS.
[1740—1815.]

AN EVENING HYMN.

THE moon hath risen clear,
The golden stars appear,
In heaven that o'er us bendeth;
Dark, still the forest stands,
And from the meadow-lands
The strange, white mist ascendeth.

How calmly hill and dale
Lie in the twilight's veil,
That round them softly closes!
Like to a chamber still,

Where, after daylight's ill,
The heart in sleep reposes.

See you the moon arise?
But half behold our eyes,
Yet perfect is her being.
Thus many things may be
We mock at carelessly
For want of better seeing.

God! let us know thy light,
Trust in no vain delight,
Desire no fleeting treasure:
Let us in virtue grow,
That we may here below
With guiltless childhood measure.

And when our life is past,
May unto us at last

A peaceful death be given.

Then mayest Thou us bring,

Our Father and our King,

Unto Thy holy heaven.

Now, brethren, seek your rest

By God's protection blest.

The night grows chill and dreary:

From ill may God us keep,

To us give quiet sleep,

And to the sick and weary.

THE LOST STAR.

There stood a star in the heavens,

.A star of brightness rare,

So lovely was its radiance,

So tender and so fair.

'Midst all the stars of heaven
  Full well I knew its place,
I sought it in the evening
  Till I its light could trace.

And long I stood there gazing
  With ever-fresh delight,
To watch that star arising,
  And thank God every night.

The star it shines no longer,
  I seek it o'er and o'er,
Where I was wont to find it,
  And find it now no more.

THE SPRING.

ON THE FIRST MAY MORNING.

To-day will I rejoice, rejoice, rejoice,

List to nought that form and custom say;

Gaily dance and raise in song my voice,

And no king on earth shall bid me stay.

For with all his joys, o'er hills and vales,

Forth he cometh from the realms of morn;

On his shoulders sit the nightingales,

Flowers his breast and golden locks adorn.

Dews and blessings sheds he on his way,

In his face the rose and lily meet;

Ha! my Thyrsus is a budding spray,

And I hasten forth my friend to greet.

LUDWIG H. C. HÖLTY.
[1748-1776.]

SONG.

Who would his life with troubles weary,
While youth and spring-time brightly bloom?
Or who, while in his days of gladness,
Would cloud his brow with shades of gloom?

Joy beckons us on ev'ry pathway,
Crossing this pilgrim life of ours;
And when we're at the crossway standing,
She offers us the wreath of flowers.

Still through the meadows flows the brooklet,
Still is the arbour cool and green,
And still the moon shines forth as brightly
As erst through Eden's trees 'twas seen.

Still heals the grape, with juice of purple,
The human heart of ev'ry care;
And sweet is, in the evening twilight,
The kiss upon lips rosy-fair.

The nightingale stills wakes at even
Enchantment in the youthful breast,
And still her song with balmy sweetness
Unto the stricken soul gives rest.

Oh! wondrous fair is God's creation,
And full of gladness unto me!
Then till I sink to dust and ashes,
Will I rejoice, fair earth, in thee.

FRIEDRICH L. von STOLBERG.

[1750-1819.]

THE MOUNTAIN TORRENT.

UNDYING youth,
'Forth streamest thou
From the rocky cleft.
No mortal hath seen
The strong one's first cradle;
No ear ever heard
The noble one's lisping in spray-tossing fountains.
How fair art thou, fair
In thy silvery tresses!
How fearful art thou
In the thunder of echoing rocks!

Thou shakest the fir-tree,

O'erthrowest the fir-tree

With root and with branch.

The rocks would flee from thee,

Thou holdest them firmly;

Like pebbles thou castest them from thee in sport.

Thou'rt clothed by the sun

In his glorious rays;

He paints, with the hues of the heavenly rainbow,

The hovering clouds of the spray-covered flood.

Why hastenest thou

To the emerald sea?

Art thou not happy thus nearer to heaven?

In echoing rocks, in the oak trees o'erhanging!

Oh, hasten not thus

To the emerald sea!

Youth, thou art yet as strong as a god,

Free as a god!

Though smile there beneath thee the rest and the stillness,

The sea in its silence, its trembling emotion,

Now silvered by soft-falling moonbeams,

Now crimson and gold in the rays of the west.

Oh youth! what availeth the silken reposing?

What is the smile that the moonbeam bestoweth,

The sunset's radiance of purple and gold,

To him who in fetters of slavery dwells?

    Still streamest thou wild

    As thy heart commands.

Beneath thee, oft winds ever fickle are reigning,

Oft stillness of death in the time-serving sea.

    Oh, hasten not thus

    To the emerald sea!

Youth, thou art yet as strong as a god,

    Free as a god!

JOHANN WOLFGANG von GOETHE.

[1749-1832.]

MIGNON.

Oh ! let me seem until in truth I be !
   The snow-white dress, oh, let me keep !
For soon I from this beauteous earth must flee
   Down to yon house secure and deep.

There shall my rest a little while endure,
   Till I behold a brighter day ;
Then shall I lay aside this raiment pure,
   The wreath and girdle cast away.

And nought those beings cast in heav'nly mould
  Of man and woman heed or know,
And never earthly robes and garments' fold
  Around their radiant bodies flow.

Though free I lived from toil and anxious fears,
  I have enough of grief and pain :
'Tis sorrow ages me before my years ;
  Make me for ever young again !

THE FISHER.

The water swelled, the water rose,
  A fisher sat anear,
Gazed at his float in calm repose,
  Calm as the waters clear ;
And as he sits and listens there,
  He sees the floods divide,

A foam-besprinkled maiden fair
Arises from the tide.

She sang to him, she spoke to him,
' Ah ! why my children call,
With human cunning, human wit,
In deadly glow to fall ?
The fishes' joy, oh ! couldst thou tell
Our ocean depths within,
Thou wouldst come down with us to dwell,
Here perfect health to win.

' Do not the sun and moon too lave
Themselves in ocean main,
Returning breathing of the wave,
All doubly fair again ?
Say charmeth thee not heaven's space,
The blue of liquid light ?

Say, charmeth thee not thine own face
In dew for ever bright?'

The water swelled, the water rose,
It laps his naked feet;
His heart with longing overflows,
As though his love to greet:
She spoke to him, she sang to him,
Then all for him was o'er;
She drew him half, he half sank in,
And none beheld him more.

———

A WANDERER'S EVENING SONG.

THOU who from the heavens art,
Ev'ry pain and sorrow stilling,
Still the doubly wretched heart,
Doubly with refreshment filling—

Would that all this toil might cease!

Why this joy and grief's unrest?

  Gentle peace!

Come, oh, come into my breast!

ANOTHER.

Rest o'er all the summits

  Is now,

In all the tree-tops

  Feelest thou

No breath of wind.

Each bird sleeps in its nest:

Oh! wait a while—rest

  Thou too wilt find.

DEDICATION.

The morning came, his footsteps swiftly chasing
The slumber, calm and light, wherein I lay;
And I awakened, from my lowly dwelling
Went gaily forth upon the mountain way.
At ev'ry step my heart with joy was swelling
To mark the dew-bespangled budding spray;
The youthful day with joy himself upreared,
And to refresh me all refreshed appeared.

And as I clomb, from forth the meadow river
A mist in dappled streaks all softly sped:
It moved, and, changefully around me flowing,
It rose with wingéd swiftness o'er my head.
No more I watched the scene with beauties glowing,
A mournful veil was o'er the landscape spread;

Soon clouds on ev'ry side around me played,
And I was wrapped in twilight's gloomy shade.

Here suddenly the sun appeared returning,
For through the misty veil was seen a light;
Now softly sank the cloud, beneath me meeting,
Now parting, rose to soar o'er wood and height.
Fain would I bring his rays the earliest greeting,
Fain see him after darkness doubly bright.
Still raged the airy strife, above, below, .
When I was dazzled by a sudden glow.

Soon by my inmost heart's desires emboldened,
I ventured once again mine eyes to raise:
I could but take one glance around and o'er me,
For all appeared to be one glowing blaze.
When floating, borne upon the clouds before me,
A god-like woman met my wond'ring gaze:

No fairer e'er beheld my raptured sight:
She looked on me, and stayed her even flight.

'Know'st thou me not?' she said, in accents breathing
Of faithfulness and love in ev'ry strain.
'Know'st thou me not, whose hand a balsam vernal
Poured oft to heal thy life of many a pain!
Thou know'st me well, to whom in vows eternal
Thy striving heart to bind itself were fain.
Oft have I seen thee in thy boyhood's years,
Oft yearning after me with eager tears.'

'Yes!' I exclaimed, in blissful wonder sinking
Upon the ground, 'I felt thee long ago;
Thou gav'st me rest when passion's torrent wildly
Too often through my youthful limbs did flow.
'Tis thou who, like the breath of heaven, mildly,
Has cooled my fevered brow at noonday glow.

The earth's best gifts thou hast bestowed on me,
And ev'ry joy I'll know alone through thee.

'I name thee not, though I hear many utter
Thy name, and each one claims thee for his own.
To many an eye thy rays bring shame and terror,
Yet all believe thy light for them hath shone.
Friends were around me in my days of error,
Now that I know thee, I am nigh alone.
I must alone enjoy my treasured prize;
Thy gracious light conceal from other eyes.'

She smiled, she said : 'Thou seest 'twas wise and
    needful
By slow degrees my knowledge to distil :
For scarce from gross deception freed thou seemest,
Scarce hast o'ermastered childhood's early will,

When more than human thou thyself esteemest,
Neglectest human duties to fulfil.
Dost thou above thy brothers think to rise?
Know thou thyself, nor thus the world despise.'

'Forgive me,' I exclaimed, 'I thought no evil;
Didst thou in vain thy light to me reveal?
A joyous will hath all my heart inspired,
The value of thy precious gifts I feel:
For others I the noble boon desired,
No longer I the treasure will conceal.
Why should I labour thus the path to find,
If not to show it unto all mankind?'

And as I spoke, with looks of mild indulgence
Upon me gazed that lofty being bright;
And in her eyes I could myself discover
Where error I had sought, and where the right.

She smiled, and all my ills as soon were over;
My spirit rose and soared to new delight.
I dared, now confidently drawing near,
To gaze upon her, free from doubt and fear.

Then forth she stretched her hand, the streaks dividing
Of clouds and dew that hung the valley o'er.
Whate'er she grasped, her gentle touch obeying,
Her hand could draw it, there was mist no more.
Mine eyes again o'er all the landscape straying,
Beheld the heavens cloudless, as before.
But in her hand the purest veil she held,
That in a thousand folds around her swelled.

'I know thee well, I know thy ev'ry weakness;
The good that in thee lives is known to me'—
These were her words, I hear her speak for ever—
'Receive now what I destined long for thee.

Thrice happy he, and lacking blessings never,

Who takes this gift with peaceful soul and free:

Of air and sunshine woven, take, O youth!

The veil of poetry from the hand of truth.

'And when thy friends and thou grow faint and weary,

Then fling it in the air at noonday's glow,

And evening breezes, cool around you stealing,

The breath of sweet and balmy flow'rs will blow;

Assuaged is ev'ry painful earthly feeling,

And changed to beds of clouds the grave below;

The waves of life all smooth and still appear,

The day grows lovely and the night grows clear.'

Then come, my friends, when on your pathway ever

The cares of life are fast and faster borne;

Or when your path returning blessings daily

With flowers deck, with golden fruits adorn;

United all, we meet the morrow gaily,

And wander joyously from morn to morn;

And when our children shall our loss deplore,

Our love shall be their joy for evermore.

THE VIOLET.

A VIOLET on the lea did grow,

Unknown and humbly bent full low;

It was a lovely flower.

There came a maiden young and fair,

With heart and footsteps light as air,

Across, across the lea with merry song.

'Ah!' thought the violet, 'could I be

The fairest blossom on the lea,

Ah, but for one short hour!
My love might pluck me with a smile,
And press me to her heart the while,
Though but, though but, a few swift moments long.'

Alas! she came, the maiden fair,
And of the violet took no care,—
She crushed the little flower;
It sank and died, rejoiced to die,
' And though I perish, yet I die
Through her, through her, and at her feet I lie !'

THE LOVED ONE NEAR.

I THINK of thee when sunshine bright is streaming
    On ocean deeps;
I think of thee when moonlight, softly beaming,
    On fountains sleeps.

I see thee, when on mountain path of danger
        The dust doth play;
In darksome night when trembling goes the stranger
        His narrow way.

I hear thee when, with muffled roaring, yonder
        The torrents swell;
And list'ning, oft when all is still, I wander
        In quiet dell.

I am with thee; though thou afar art roaming,
        To me thou'rt near;
The sun has set, the stars shine through the gloaming;
        Oh! wert thou here!

THE MINSTREL.

'Upon the bridge, without the door,
What sounds fall on mine ear?
Go, let the song be sung once more
Within my palace here.'
The monarch spoke, the page he sped,
The boy returned, the monarch said:
'Bring in the aged ministrel.'

'God greet ye well, ye noble knights,
God greet ye well, fair dames;
What heaven, rich with starry lights!
Who telleth me their names?
This hall of splendour and of power—
Be closed, mine eyes, 'tis not the hour
To gaze in wond'ring pleasure.'

He closed his eyes, the minstrel old,

And woke a stirring air,

Up looked the knights right brave and bold,

And down each lady fair.

The king, well pleased with what he sang,

Bade one around his neck to hang

A chain of gold as guerdon.

' Give not to me the golden chain !

The gift thy knights may take,

Before whose ranks on battle plain

The hostile lances break.

Give it thy Chancellor of State,

That he may bear the golden weight

Besides his other burdens.

' I sing, as sings the bird whose home

Is in the air so free ;

The songs forth from my throat that come
Are sweet reward for me.
Yet dare I beg, this boon be mine,
Give me the cup of purest wine
Within a golden goblet.'

He raised the cup, he drank it dry:
' Oh, cordial pure and bright !
Oh ! house thrice blessed with blessings high
That holds such boon as slight !
When ye are happy think of me,
And thank your God as earnestly,
As for this cup I thank you.'

A HARPER'S SONG.

Who never weeping ate his bread,
Who never through the midnight hours

Sat sore lamenting on his bed;

He knows ye not, ye heav'nly powers!

Ye lead us to this life below,

Ye leave the wretch in sin to fall,

Then ye abandon him to woe,

Since all sins do for vengeance call.

TO MIGNON.

Over stream and vale away

Floats the golden car of day;

Ah! its course, o'er wood and plain,

Makes thy griefs and mine to dart

Through my heart,

As each morning wakes again.

Night scarce bringeth me repose;

For whene'er mine eyes I close,

Mournful dreams my sleep affright,
And I feel the pangs that dart
Through my heart,
Strengthen, deepen night by night.

Oft in happy years have I
Watched the ships go sailing by,
All towards their harbour glide;
But, alas! the pangs that dart
Through my heart,
Pass not with the river's tide.

I must wear my gayest dress,
Taken from the shelved recess,
For the festival to-day.
No one knows the pangs that dart
Through my heart,
Fiercely tearing it away.

Ceaseless falls the hidden tear,

But contented I appear,

E'en my cheek a healthful red.

Did these pangs with fatal dart

Pierce my heart,

Ah! long since I had been dead.

THE WEDDING SONG.

We love to remember and sing you the lay

Of the Count, who resided of old

In the castle, wherein for his grandson to-day

The wedding rejoicings ye hold.

It chanced that the former in Palestine's land

Had won many laurels in warlike command;

And when he again at his threshold did stand,

He found there his castle alone,

But servants and property flown.

Now, Count, hast returned to thy castle once more,

But changes full many are there;

The winds through the casements they whistle and roar,

And into the chambers so bare.

What now can be done, in the cold autumn night?

Full many I've passed in a heavier plight,

And brighter all grows with the dawning of light;

Then quick, by the moonbeams o'erhead,

To straw, to stable, to bed.

And as all inclining to slumber he lay,

A movement he hears on the ground:

A rat at its pleasure may rustle and play,

As if it some bread crumbs had found.

But see where there standeth the tiniest wight!

A dwarf, fairly shapen, with lantern so bright,

With eloquent gestures and manners polite,

At the feet of that Count, sorely tired,
Who slumber most truly desired.

'We've ventured, Sir Count, in your castle to feast,
Since you went the Moslems to fight;
And as we believed you afar in the East,
Our revels were fixed for to-night.
And if you permit it, and know not of fear,
The dwarfs they will revel right merrily here,
Our fair little bride at her wedding to cheer.'
The Count in his dream, calm and still,
'Make use of my chamber at will.'

Then forth came three riders, careering about,
Who under the bedstead had been;
Then follows a chorus with song and with shout,
And quaintest of figures and mien.

And waggons and waggons with luxuries rare

That none but the dwellings of royalty share,

That seeing and hearing scarce credit we dare,

At last in a carriage of gold

The bride and the guests we behold.

Anon through the chamber they speedily hie,

And each tries to find him a place;

To waltz and to reel, and to gallop they fly,

The dance with their fair ones to grace.

They whistle and pipe, and they fiddle and ring,

They circle and sweep, and they rustle and swing,

They whisper and murmur, and chatter and sing :

The Count, as he gazed on the scene,

Himself in a fever did ween.

Now rappings and tappings and clappings resound

Of benches and tables and chairs,

And each to the feast drawing merrily round,

A seat by his lady prepares.

They bear in the ham and the sausages small,

The venison, the fish, and the poultry and all;

The costliest wine flows at ev'ry one's call;

They frolic and revel so long,

And vanish at last with a song.

And shall I the rest of the story make known?

Then frolic and noise must be stilled,

For what by the dwarfs was so pleasantly shown,

Himself hath enjoyed and fulfilled.

With trumpets and singing, and chariots gay,

With horses, and riders, and bridal array,

They come, and they bow, and their grandeur display,

An endless rejoicing, and revelling train:

Thus it happened, and happens again and again.

FRIEDERICH von SCHILLER.
[1759—1805.]

THE LAMENT OF CERES.*

Is the joyous spring-time nearing?
Has the earth grown young again?
Verdant are the hills appearing,
Broken is the icy chain.
In the streamlet's mirror brightly
Laughs the blue unclouded sky,
Zephyr's pinions flit more lightly,
And the budding plants grow high;
Through the woods the birds are singing,
And the Dryad speaks to me;

---

* In this, as in the other classical poems of Schiller, I have followed his example of using indifferently the Greek and Roman names of gods, &c.

All thy flow'rs the year is bringing,
Not thy daughter unto thee!

Ah! how long I've wandered sadly!
O'er all earth my way I wend.
Titan, all thy rays how gladly
On the precious track I'd send.
Never one to me unfoldeth
Tidings of the lovèd face;
And the day, who all beholdeth,
Of my lost one sees no trace.
From my side didst, Zeus, thou tear her?
Or, enamoured of her charms,
Did to Hades Pluto bear her
Captive in his dusky arms?

Who to yonder gloomy river
Will my tale of sorrow bear?

Though the boat is passing ever,
None but shades may enter there.
Closed to ev'ry eye immortal,
Still the Stygian waters roll;
Never yet has Hades' portal
Opened to a living soul.
Many paths to yonder dwelling
Lead, but none return to light.
Of her tears no witness telling
Comes to greet the mother's sight.

Mothers earthly-born, descended
From the Phrygians' mortal race,
Through the grave, when life is ended,
May their child once more embrace.
Only those who dwell in heaven
Never near the darksome strand;

Only to the blest is given,

Fates! exemption from your hand.

Cast me into night for ever

From Olympus' golden day;

Heed the rights of goddess never,

Ah! the mother's torture they!

Where, beside stern Pluto sitting,

Joyless state she keeps, I'd fly;

With the noiseless shadows flitting

To the monarch's throne draw nigh.

Ah! her eyes, with tears o'erstreaming,

Seek in vain the golden light;

Of a distant region dreaming,

Meet they not the mother's sight;

Till by joy made known, united

Heart to heart once more can be,

And to sympathy excited,

Even Orcus weeps to see.

Vain lament ! sighs unavailing !

In the self-same even train

Rolls the car of day unfailing,

Zeus' decrees unchanged remain ;

Far from yonder land of shadows

Bright and happy moveth he.

Once within those sunless meadows,

She is ever lost to me,

Till the Styx' dark waters brightly

With Aurora's colours glow,

And through Hades Iris lightly

Draws her ever-changing bow.

Have I then no tender token,

No remembrance sweet that tells

Love, though parted, 's still unbroken,
Though so far from me she dwells?
Can no links of true love ever
Yet unite my child to me?
'Twixt the dead and living never
Can a bond of union be?
No, they did not quite bereave me!
No! she is not wholly ta'en!
Since the high immortals leave me
One communion for us twain.

When the flow'rs of spring are dying,
When, by winter's icy air
Faded, scattered leaves are lying,
And the trees stand sad and bare,
Then the life of all the living
Take I from Vertumnus' horn,

To the realms of darkness giving
Sacrifice of golden corn.
In the earth 'tis laid with sorrow,
Laid beside my darling's heart,
That a language there it borrow,
Grief and love for me impart.

When the Horae, reappearing,
Lead the spring-time in their train,
And the sunbeams, bright and cheering,
Rouse the dead to life again,
Germs that death-like long had slumbered
In the chilly lap of earth,
To the realm of hues unnumbered
With rejoicing hasten forth;
While the stems arise towards heaven,
Seek the timid roots the night;

To the mingled care they're given

Of the Styx and ether's might.

Half among the dead they're dwelling,

Half they touch the living land,

Unto me sweet tidings telling,

Voices from Cocytus' strand.

Though herself he captive holdeth

In the abyss of darkness drear,

From the buds that spring unfoldeth

Still her gentle words I hear,

That, though far from daylight's greeting,

Where the mournful shadows go,

Still with love the hearts are beating,

Warmly still the spirits glow.

Be ye welcomed then with pleasure,

Children of the meadow born,

I will fill your cups with treasure

Of the clearest dews of morn.

Ye shall bathe in sunbeams glowing

With the rainbow's purest light;

I will paint your petals, growing

Like Aurora, fair and bright.

In the spring-time's cheerful splendour,

In the autumn's faded leaf,

Readeth ev'ry bosom tender

All my joy and all my grief.

THE FISHER-BOY.

THE lake is asleep, and smiles in its sleeping,

The boy on the shore his rest is keeping,

    He hears a ringing

      Like flutes arise,

Like angels singing

In Paradise.

And when in his bliss he awakens from rest,

The wavelets are playing around his breast;

It sounds from the waters,

' Fair boy, mine thou'lt be;

I lure down the sleeper,

I draw him to me.'

DESIRE.

Oh! from out this valley dreary,

By a chilly mist opprest,

Could I flee, though weak and weary,

Oh, how greatly I were blest!

Pleasant hills I see before me,
Ever young and green they lie;
Had I pinions that upbore me,
Swiftly to those hills I'd fly.

Thence harmonious music ringeth,
Peace like heaven, calm and sweet;
Balsam-laden odours bringeth
Unto me the zephyr fleet.
Golden fruits, their splendour glowing,
'Midst their glossy leaves display;
And the flowers, that there are growing,
Ne'er become the winter's prey.

Ah! in sunshine bright, eternal,
Sweet must be to wander there;
And on yonder summit vernal,
Oh, how pure must be the air!

But I fear the stormy river,
That in anger flows between;
Its uplifted billows ever
Fill my soul with terrors keen.

Lo! a bark the shore is nearing,
But, alas! the helmsman fails;
Boldly enter, nothing fearing,
And inspired thou'lt find the sails.
Faith and courage! these must speed thee,
For the gods will pledge no sign;
Nought but wonders e'er can lead thee
To that wonderland divine!

THE FEAST OF VICTORY.

FALLEN had Ilion, famed in story,
Troy in dust and ruin lay;

And the Greeks, elate with glory,

Richly laden with their prey,

Toward their lofty ships were faring

On the Hellespontine strand,

For the joyful course preparing

To their beauteous fatherland.

 Sing ye then a gladsome strain,

 For our ships with merry cheer

 To our native shore we steer,

 And our homes we seek again.

And in sorrow unavailing,

Sat the Trojan maidens fair;

Beat their breasts, with sighs and wailing;

Pale, with all unbraided hair.

In the feast of gladness blending,

Their lament rang mournfully,

For their country's greatness ending,
And their own captivity.

    Land, farewell! beloved the best;
    Far upon a foreign shore
    We must bow the foe before;
    Ah! the dead in truth are blest.

Now to each celestial being,
Calchas bids the incense rise;
And on Pallas, who all-seeing
Founds the city, first he cries;
Neptune, who his band of ocean,
Circling round all countries flings;
Zeus, who swift with lightning motion,
High the fearful Ægis swings.

    Ended are the years of pain,
    Din of arms is heard no more,

For the time of strife is o'er,
And the mighty city ta'en.

Now the Grecian leader sadly
Counteth o'er the army's tale,
That had followed him so gladly
Once from the Scamander's vale.
And the clouds of sorrow lower
Deeply o'er the monarch's brow;
Of his people's pride and power
Little there remaineth now.
 Sing ye then the joyful strain,
 Ye who still, all brave and bright,
 Seek once more your home's delight,
 For not all return again.

Nor by all, though home returning,
Is a joyous welcome shared;

By the household altar burning,

Oft may murder be prepared.

Many fell when friends conspired,

Who from battle safely came,

Warning spoke Ulysses, fired

By Athene's prophet-flame.

    Happy he whose wife remains

    Faithful to the absent e'er ;

    Woman still is false and fair,

    All that's new her fancy gains.

In his wife, reconquered newly,

Greatly joys the Spartan king;

Round that fair form praised so truly

Doth his arm rejoicing fling.

Evil doings prosper never,

Still revenge must follow crime,

For celestial justice ever
Sits in heavenly heights sublime.
    Evil deed hath evil end.
    Zeus from out the highest place
    Vengeance on the impious race,
    Takes for th' injured host and friend.

' For the happy 'tis befitting,'
Thus the mighty Ajax spoke,
' Those on heaven's throne who're sitting,
For their justice to invoke.
But in wild confusion hurried,
Pour the gifts from fortune's urn ;
For Patrocles lieth buried,
While Thersites doth return.
    Since, then, fortune's favours run
    Blindly mingled, careless, free,

Great let his rejoicing be
Who the lot of life has won.

' Yes ! war robs us of our dearest,
We remember thee for aye ;
When the wine-cups ring the clearest,
Thou a shield in battle fray.
'Twas thine arm that stayed the danger
When the flames our vessels gained ;
Craft alone, to thee a stranger,
Has so fair a prize attained.
   May in peace thine ashes rest,
   Thou not stricken in the fight ;
   Ajax fell by Ajax' might,
   Discord still destroys the best.'

Now unto his mighty sire,
Pyrrhus poureth high the wine,

Say, what lot can praise inspire,
Noble father, like to thine?
Of all gifts that man enjoyeth,
Highest evermore is fame;
E'en when death the clay destroyeth,
Still survives a noble name.
 Hero! in the minstrel's strain
 Deathless shall thy glory be;
 For our earthly moments flee,
 And the dead alone remain.

Since no voice the mourner raises,
Telling of the vanquished man,
I will sing of Hector's praises.
Thus Tydeus' son began,
Who his household altars shielded,
Falling on the field of fame,

Spite of crowns to victors yielded,.
His is still the loftier aim.
    Who in mortal combat fell
    For his household altar's fame,
    Long the honour of his name,
    E'en the foeman's lips shall tell.

Nestor now, that warrior olden,
Who a threefold life has seen,
Gives the wreathèd wine-cup golden
Unto Priam's weeping queen :
' Drink the cordial that I proffer,
And thy bitter anguish calm :
Wondrous gifts doth Bacchus offer,
To the wounded heart a balm.
    Drink the cordial sparkling bright,
    And thy bitter anguish calm !

To the wounded heart a balm,
Bacchus' gift hath wondrous might.'

Niobe in terror shrinking,
Of celestial wrath the aim,
Even she, the cordial drinking,
Deepest sorrow overcame.
While the cup of life is glowing
At the lips of those who mourn,
Deep in Lethe's river flowing,
Swiftly hence their grief is borne.

 While the cup of life yet glows
 At the lips of those who mourn,
 Swiftly hence their grief is borne
 By the stream that darkly flows.

Now the prophetess has risen,
The divine, inspired maid,

Gazing from her floating prison

On her home in ashes laid.

Vain is all our earthly glory;

Like the vapour's wind-rocked train,

Fadeth hence our life's brief story,

And the gods alone remain.

    Round the horse and rider gay,

    Round the ship float grief and care;

    Ours is not the morrow's share,

    Let us therefore live to-day.

DITHRYAMBE.

NEVER the gods thou beholdest,

    Believe me,

    Never alone!

Scarcely that Bacchus, the mirthful one, neareth,

Light laughing cupid as swiftly appeareth,

Phœbus descends from his heavenly throne.

 The beings celestial

 Are nearing me all;

 And gods are approaching

 The earthly-built hall.

How shall I welcome—

 I, human creature—

 The heavenly band?

Gods! let me enter eternity's portal.

What can he give you whose life is but mortal?

Bear me with you to Olympus' bright land.

 With Jupiter only

 Can happiness be!

 O! pour out the nectar,

 O! give it to me!

His be the goblet!

 Pour for the poet,

 Hebe, the wine!

Sprinkle his eyelids with heaven's dew glowing,

That he behold not the Styx darkly flowing;

Like unto us, he may deem him divine.

 The fountain celestial

 Pours forth, sparkling bright;

 The eye groweth clearer,

 The heart groweth light.

THE GODS OF GREECE.

When the fair and sunny earth ye governed,

Leading it by pleasure's easy hand,

Happy generations then ye guided,

Beauteous beings from a fabled land.

Ah! while yet your blissful worship flourished,

What a mystic golden past was there,

While they garlanded thy temple daily,

Venus Amathusia fair!

When the witching veil of fancy ever

Sought truth's naked sternness to conceal,

Life's abundance flowed through all creation,

And that felt which never yet could feel.

Nature, thus for love's embraces fitter,

All ennobled was, and lived and glowed,

All to understanding eyes the traces

Of celestial footsteps showed.

Where now, as our sages fain would teach us,

Turns a fiery ball, devoid of soul,

Helios then, majestically placid,

Drove his golden car from pole to pole.

Sylvan nymphs abode in yonder mountain,
Every tree became a Dryad's home.
From the urns of lovely Naiads flowing
Sprang the fountain's silver foam.

Yonder laurel once implored assistance;
Niobe was silenced in yon stone:
Syrinx' wailings in the sedge resounded;
Through this wood rang Philomela's moan.
Yonder brook hath Ceres' tears collected,
That she for Persephone let fall;
From these heights would oft Cytherea vainly
On her fair belovéd call.

To the race of man awhile descending,
The immortals their abode forsook;
And to gain the love of Pyrrhus' daughter,
Leto's son assumed the shepherd's crook.

Mortal men and gods and mighty heroes,

Love united in a blissful band;

Mortals thus with gods and heroes worshipped,

In the Amathusian land.

Dark and stern asceticism never

Was received your cheerful forms within;

Ev'ry heart to beat with joy was bidden,

For the happy were to you akin.

Nought besides the beautiful was holy,

Never then with shame a god retired,

From enjoyment which the chaste Camenæ,

Or Euphrosyne desired.

Like to palaces appeared your temples,

In your honour was the heroes' game

In the Isthmean feasts, the many-crowned,

When the victor's chariot thund'ring came.

Fair-entwining, soul-inspiring dances
Circled round your splendid altar stair;
Round your brows were wreathed the victor's garlands,
Crowns adorned your fragrant hair.

Merry Thyrsus-bearers' salutations,
And the panther steeds in proud array,
These announced the mighty pleasure-bringer;
Fawns and satyrs reeling led the way.
Round him whirl the wildly savage Mænads,
In their dances they his wine extol,
And the host's embrownéd cheeks and ruddy
Summon to the festal bowl.

Then appeared no dark and gloomy spectre
At the dying mortal's couch of woe;
In a kiss the breath of life departed,
And the spirit's torch burns dim and low.

Even Hades' scales of justice fearful
Were suspended from a mortal hand;
And the Thracian's soul-inspiring wailings
Moved the Furies' dreadful band.

Happy shades their ev'ry earthly pleasure
In Elysian fields enjoyed again;
True love met once more the faithful husband,
Chariot-leaders found the racing plain.
Linus' voice in well-known songs resoundeth,
Round his wife his arms Admetus throws,
There Orestes by his friend is greeted,
And the archer grasps his bows.

Higher prizes then the wrestlers strengthened
On the course of virtue's toilsome road;
Noble heroes of great actions slowly
Climbed into th' immortals' blest abode.

Lowly there before the dead's reclaimer,
Bent the hosts divine all silently;
And the mighty Twins the pilot guided
From Olympus o'er the sea.

Beauteous world, where art thou? Nature's fairest,
Brightest spring-time, oh, come back, come back!
Only in the fairy-land of poetry
Yet existeth here thy fabled track.
No divinity my gaze beholdeth,
Barren mourn the wide, deserted plains:
Of the picture, warm with life and glowing,
'Tis the shadow that remains.

Faded all these blossoms are and scattered,
By the north wind's chill and dreary blast;
To enrich a single one, this kingdom
Of the gods must fade into the past.

Sadly search I 'midst the stars unnumbered;

Thou, Selene, there no more art found;

Through the woods I call, and through the billows—

Empty echoes thence resound.

All unconscious of the joys she gives us,

By their beauty never more impressed,

Knowing not the mighty soul that guides her,

Never by my blissfulness more blest;

Careless of her great Creator's honour,

Dull, mechanically, line by line,

Servilely, to heavy laws she bows her

Nature, now no more divine.

She to-day herself her tomb prepareth,

On the morrow thence to rise again;

And the moons, in one unchanging circle,

Ever wind their self-revolving chain.

Idly to the poet's land returning,

Fled from earth the gods, now useless grown,

To a world that, from their guidance passing,

Self-sustaining, floats alone.

They returnéd home, and we of beauty

And of loftiness were all bereft;

Of life's harmony and blending colours,

Nought but soulless words to us were left.

Drawn from time's devouring flood in safety,

On Pindarian heights they float sublime;

All in life must perish that would ever

Live in song through deathless time.

THE YOUTH AT THE BROOK.

At the brook the youth was sitting
Twining wreaths of flowers gay,
And he saw them swiftly carried
In the wavelets' dance away.

'Thus, alas! my days are passing
As the restless water flows;
Like the flowers swiftly fading,
Pale and sad my spring-time grows.

'Ask not, ask not why I sorrow
In my lifetime's early spring;
All rejoice and all are hoping
For the gifts that time may bring.

But all nature's thousand voices
That are waking from their sleep,
In my inmost heart awaken
Nought but woe and sorrow deep.

'What avail the varied pleasures
That the spring has brought to me?
Near is one that I am seeking,
Yet for ever far must be.

  Still my arms I spread with longing
  Towards that shadow-image fair;
  Ah! I never can attain it,
  And my heart is full of care.

'Come, O come, thou perfect fair one,
From thy stately halls descend,
Flowers that the spring has born us
In thy lap their hues shall blend.'

  Hark! the wood resounds with singing,
  And the stream flows silver fair:
  Room is in the smallest dwelling
  For a happy, loving pair.

THE COUNT OF HABSBURG.

At Aachen, in imperial state,
  Within his castle old,
The noble Emp'ror Rudolf sate,
  A royal feast to hold.
The dishes carried the Count of the Rhine,
The Bohemian poured out the sparkling wine,
  And the seven Electors all,
As the host of stars round the sun are seen,
To do their office with loyal mien,
  Awaited their sovereign's call.

And the people filled, an exulting crowd,
  The balcony on high;
And gaily mingled the trumpets loud
  With the throng's rejoicing cry.

For the bloody wars were o'er and past,
And after years of horror at last
   A judge is over the land.
No longer ruleth the iron spear,
No longer the peaceful and weak need fear
   The lawless oppressor's hand.

And the Emperor spoke in joyous mood,
   As the goblet of gold he seized:
'The feast is bright, and the banquet good,
   And my royal heart is pleased.
But the bard I miss, who contentment brings,
Who moves the heart, as he touches the strings
   With sentiments high and divine.
From my youth have I owned the minstrel's might,
And what I enjoyed as a simple knight,
   As Emperor still shall be mine.'

And now behold! at the royal command,
    The long-robed bard appears;
He holds his harp with a trembling hand,
    And his hair is white with years.
'Sweet music sleeps in the golden strings
Of love's bright guerdon the minstrel sings.
    He praises the highest and best
That the heart can wish or the soul desire.
But say what theme can my harp inspire
    To grace the royal behest?'

And the Emperor smiled, as he thus began:
    'The bard owns not my power;
He bows to one far higher than man,
    He obeys the inspiring hour.
For as through the air the whirlwinds blow,
And whence they have risen none e'er can know,

As the spring from the hidden deep,
From the heart resoundeth the minstrel's song,
And wakens the feelings, a mystic throng
   Which have lain in a wondrous sleep.'

And the minstrel struck on the chords with might,
   And thus he commenced his lay:
' Abroad to the chase went a noble knight,
   The fleet-footed chamois to slay;
The squire behind with his weapons rode,
And as his steed a meadowland broad
   Was moving full lightly o'er,
The sounds of a bell his hearing crossed:
A priest it was with the holy Host,
   The sacristan walked before.

' Then the Count his noble head did bare,
   And reverently inclined

With Christian faith to adore in prayer
The Saviour of mankind.
A brooklet here through the meadow sped,
The torrent had flooded its tranquil bed;
The wanderer, seeing it, stayed;
The sacrament quickly he laid aside,
And, stooping low, his sandals untied,
That he through the stream might wade.

' " What doest thou there?" the Count began,
Who wondering near him stood.
" I hasten, Sir Knight, to a dying man,
Who longs for the heavenly food :
And as the ford I hastily neared,
I found it had wholly disappeared,
Destroyed by the torrent fleet.
To save the sinner my aim must be,

And I through the waters hastily,

   Must wade with my naked feet."

' Then the knight bade him mount on his noble steed,

   And gave him the bridle gay,

To relieve the penitent's utmost need,

   Nor his holy duty delay.

And he on his follower's palfrey still,

Pursued the chamois from hill to hill,

   The priest on his journey sped,

And early next morning again was seen,

Bringing back to the Count, with thankful mien,

   The horse, by the bridle led.

' " Now God forbid," with humility cried

   The Count, " that I evermore

To chase or battle would dare bestride

The steed my Saviour that bore;

And if thou consent not to hold it as thine,
Then be it devoted to service divine,
  For to Him I count it given,
From whom I hold honour and earthly wealth,
And soul and body, and life and health,
  And in whom I trust in heaven."

' " Then may the Almighty, our Shield and our King,
  Who heareth the prayer of the weak,
To glory you here and hereafter bring,
  As you now His glory did seek.
You are a mighty Count, whose name
Your knightly actions have brought to fame,
  And six fair daughters you own.
Then may they," as though inspired he cried,
" Bring each a crown to your house as bride,
  And flourish through ages unknown ! " '

And long, as musing on times gone by,

    The Emperor's head was bent,

Until on meeting the minstrel's eye,

    He read there the song's intent.

The face of the priest he as speedily knew,

And hid in the mantle of purple hue

    The tears that sprang to his eyne.

And one and all on the monarch gazed,

And knew the Count whom the minstrel praised,

    And worshipped the guidance divine.

SCHMIDT von LÜBECK.

[1766-1849.]

THE STRANGER'S EVENING SONG.

I COME from o'er the mountains free,

The twilight lies on wood and sea;

I look towards the evening star,

My home it is so far, so far.

Now has the night her tent unfurled

High over God's wide sleeping world—

The world so full, I lonely all;

The world so great, and I so small.

LÜBECK.

They live in houses side by side,
And there they peacefully abide;
The stranger's staff must wander still
Across the vale, across the hill.

The morning and the evening ray
On many a quiet vale doth play;
I wander still, am full of care,
And evermore the sigh asks 'Where?'

The sun to me seems pale and cold,
The blossoms fade, and life is old,
And what they speak is empty air;
I am a stranger ev'rywhere.

Where art thou, land beloved, mine own,
Long sought for, dreamed of, never known?

The land, the land of hopeful light—
The land where bloom my roses bright?

There wander all my dreams amain,
And there my dead arise again;
The land that speaks my language dear,
And owneth all I long for here.

In dreams o'er time and space I flee,
I softly ask of flower and tree,
And still the air brings back the sound,
'Where thou art not, is gladness found.'

FRIEDERICH von MATTHISSON.
[1761-1831.]

ADELAIDE.

LONELY wanders thy friend in the garden at spring-time,
Mildly around him flows a soft and magical radiance,
That through the wavering boughs of blossom trembleth,
    Adelaide!

In the mirroring stream, in the snow of the mountains,
In the gold-bordered clouds at the daylight's declining,
In the host of the stars thine image appeareth,
    Adelaide!

Whisper the breezes of eve through the delicate
    foliage,
Silver bells of the May through the grasses are rustling,
Billows murmuring flow, and nightingales singing,
    Adelaide !

Some day, lo ! on my grave will wondrously blossom,
From out the ashes of my heart, a flower;
Plainly glimmers on each of the petals of purple,
    Adelaide !

AN EVENING LANDSCAPE.

GOLDEN light
Crowns the height.
Soft subdued, a magic glory
Lights yon wooded castle hoary.

Calm and free

Beams the sea;

With a swan-like motion sliding,

Fisher-boats to shore are gliding.

Silver sand

Heaps the strand,

Clouds now pale, now redder growing,

On the waves their hues are throwing.

Reeds enfold,

Fringed with gold,

Yonder hill the foreland bounding,

Sea-fowl wild its heights surrounding.

Poplar trees

Rock the breeze,

Oakwoods glow, a leafy cover
Interlaced the torrent over.

On the stream
Dies the gleam,
Slowly fades the evening glory
From the wooded castle hoary.

Full moonlight
Crowns the height,
Spirit-sighs haunt musically
Graves of heroes in the valley.

F. GAUDENZ von SALIS-SEEWIS.

[1762-1834.]

PSYCHE'S GRIEF.

Psyche pines in dungeon dark and dreary

For release, she longs for light in vain;

Fears and hopes, while waiting sad and weary

For a sign that fate may break her chain.

Closely bound are Psyche's airy pinions,

But all bravely, while she makes her moan,

She remembers that in grief's dominions

Grows the palm of victory alone.

Knows that from the graveyard's desolation
Flowers bloom, 'midst thorns the roses fair,
That she wins her crown by abnegation,
That her strength is steeled by bitter air.

Joy she wins by sorrows none can number,
By a dream of longing 'midst her woes;
That no rays may come to break her slumber,
Round her tree of life the shadows close.

Psyche's wail is flute-like music sighing
Round the moonlit willow branches light;
Psyche's tears the dew at sunrise lying,
And her sighs the breath of flowers at night.

Cypress shades her myrtle flowers of gladness,
Much of sorrow, much of love she knows;

Love must lead her through the parting's sadness
To the bliss of meeting's joyful close.

Bravely can she bear grief unrelenting,
Mutely bending under fate's decree;
All her joy is soul-subdued lamenting,
All her comfort mournful melody.

. . . .

Darkness veils the goal of Psyche's mission,
And those eyes, that often look through tears,
Reach not to that summit of completion
Where the mist of falsehood disappears.

LUDWIG TIECK.

[1773 - 1853.]

AUTUMN SONG.

A BIRD flew fast the field along,
And in the sunshine sang its song,
With wondrous sweet melodious lay,
' Farewell, farewell ! I fly away.
  Far, far
  I go to-day.'

I listened as the song drew near,
With strange delight, and yet with fear,

With mournful joy, with glad unrest,
Rose eager now, and sank my breast.
  Heart, heart,
Art thou with joy or grief oppressed?

But when I saw the leafless bough,
I said, 'Alas! 'tis autumn now,
The summer guests, the swallows, fly,
Perchance thus love and longing hie;
  Far, far
  With time they fly.'

But once again the sun shone bright,
And close to me the bird did light;
It saw my tears and sang to me,
'There is no winter, love, for thee;
  No, no!
Spring it is, and e'er will be.'

NIGHT.

In wailing wind, in silent night,
A wand'rer passes by;
He sighs, and moves with footsteps light,
And on the stars does cry:
' My heart is filled with anxious care,
In loneliness and woe;
Not knowing why, not knowing where,
Through joy and pain I go.
Ye golden stars, so bright and free,
Ye are for ever far from me,
   Yes, far from me,
Yet all my trust in you shall be.

And lo! a sound rings on the air,
Light on the darkness breaks;
His heart no more is weighed with care,

And all his spirit wakes.

'Oh, man! we are both far and nigh;
Thou art not lonely here.
Oh, trust to us! full oft thine eye
Has watched our light so clear.
We golden stars, so bright and free,
Are not for ever far from thee.
  For gladly we,
The golden stars, oft think of thee.'

CLEMENS BRENTANO.

[1777 - 1842.]

I SOUGHT TO BIND A POSY.

I SOUGHT to bind a posy,

But night sank o'er the lea,

And I could find no flower,

Else had I brought it thee.

My tears fell fast and faster

Into the clover sweet,

And there I saw a flower,

That blossomed at my feet.

For thee would I have plucked it

Down in the clover low,

When it began and murmured—
'Ah! do not pain me so.

'Oh! look upon me kindly,
Of thine own sorrow think;
Before my time with suff'ring
Let me not, dying, sink.'

And had it not thus spoken
Alone upon the lea,
For thee it had been gathered,
But now it may not be.

My love no longer cometh,
But lonely leaveth me :
With love still cometh sorrow,
And thus 'twill ever be.

TO SEVILLA.

To Sevilla, to Sevilla,
Where the splendid buildings stately
In the broadest streets are seen,
Noble ladies look sedately
From behind the casement screen;
'Tis not there I fain would be.

To Sevilla, to Sevilla,
Where in narrow streets are seen
Neighbours, kindly greetings sending,
And behind the casement screen
Maidens fair, their flowers tending;
There, ah, there I long to be!

In Sevilla, in Sevilla,
Is a house I know full well;

Chamber, kitchen, glisten brightly;

In that house my love doth dwell,

And the door is closed but lightly;

When I knock she lets me in.

To Sevilla, to Sevilla,

Unto her I love so dearly!

Once again I must behold her,

Hear her voice, and speak in answer,

In my arms again enfold her;

This it is my heart desires.

JOSEPH FREIHERR von EICHENDORF.

[1788-1857.]

THE BROKEN RING.

THERE turns in yon cool valley
A mill-wheel evermore;
My loved one has departed,
Who dwelt there years before.

Her troth to me she plighted,
And gave a ring thereby;
Her troth to me she's broken,
The ring doth shattered lie.

I'd fain as minstrel journey
Far through the world away;
From house to house I'd wander,
And sing my simple lay.

I'd fain fly as a rider
Into the bloody fight,
And lie around the fires,
Out in the camp at night.

And when I hear the mill-wheel turn,
I know not what I will;
To die were best meseemeth,
Then 'twere for ever still.

ABROAD.

I HEAR the brooklets murmur
As through the wood they flow,
Where 'midst the wood and murmur,
I am, I scarcely know.

The nightingales are singing
Here in the forest lone,
As though sweet tidings bringing
Of happy days long flown.

Fast speed the moonbeams flying,
As though mine eyes could see
The castle 'neath them lying,
But that is far from me.

As though my true-love roaming
'Midst roses white and red,
Must there await my coming,
But she is long since dead.

GRIEF.

'Tis true I sometimes sing,
As though 'twere well with me,
Yet secret tears soon spring,
And set my sad heart free.

E'en thus the nightingale,
Caged in the gladsome spring,
With longing's tuneful tale
  Makes all her prison ring.

Then hushed are hearts in gladness,

And listening all rejoice,

Yet none perceive what sadness

Lurks in the thrilling voice.

J. O. L.

ERNST MORITZ ARNDT.

[1769 - 1860.]

THE SOLACE OF TEARS.

Do not dry thy tears that mourn the dead!
Tears in sign of endless love are shed;
In the eyes that weep in deathless sadness
Shines reflected heaven's eternal gladness.

Check not grief for those the grave enfoldeth,
Yonder tomb thy best possessions holdeth;
All that swiftly as the wind departs,
Empty treasure was in empty hearts.

Let the dust to other dust be cast,

As thou mournest, so thy love will last;

As thou lovest, thou wilt love for ever,

E'en should sun and moon in pieces sever.

To the angels thee thy tears will bring,

And thy longings to the angels' King.

Suffer, heart, the strong o'ermastering feeling,

Heaven's future light to thee revealing.

Oh! the bliss in midst of anguish given!

Seek, oh heart! the heart of God in heaven,

In those arms that all the world embrace,

And thy sorrow unto joy gives place.

THEODOR KÖRNER.
[1791-1813.]

THE DEATH-SONG.

My deep wound burns, my lips are cold as clay,
I feel my heart's faint beating grow less clear,
A sign to me the hour of death is near—
Thy will be done, oh Lord ! my shield and stay !
I saw around me golden visions play,
That sunny dream has changed to death-wails drear.
Be strong, oh heart ! what thou didst cherish here
Will live with thee in yonder realms for aye.
And what I held on earth a sacred truth,
That kindled all the passion of my youth,

No matter if it freedom were or love,

Now as an angel radiant-fair I see,

And as my senses pass, uplifteth me

A breath to morn-illumined heights above.

TO SPRING.

HAIL, Spring, I adore thee!

Bear me, I implore thee,

With thy young life amid blossoms thriving,

With all thy hopes and thy earnest striving!

For as new life through all thy buds is thrilling,

And as each new-born blossom blooms and grows,

So all my dreams the happy spring is filling,

And through my wearied heart new power flows.

But ah ! those blossoms frail and slender,
    And those trees of living green,
All are dreams too fleet, too tender ;
    After waking, no more seen.
Drear winter soon his swift return is winging,
And then the nightingales will cease their singing,
    And joyous life sinks down with piteous sigh
    Into the grave, cold, op'ning hideously.

But little reck I of future sorrow,
    Little fear I these joys' decay ;
Spring reigns in my heart to-day and to-morrow,
    Spring in my breast endures for aye.

PRAYER DURING BATTLE.

FATHER, I call on Thee!
Darker the smoke of the battle is growing,
Round me the thunderous lightning is glowing:
God of the battle! I call on thee.
Father! oh lead Thou me!

Father! oh lead Thou me!
Whether to glory or death be my way,
Thee I acknowledge, Thy laws I obey.
Lord, as thou wilt, so lead thou me.
God! I acknowledge Thee!

God! I acknowledge Thee!
As in the rustle of leaves falling light,
So in the thunder and storm of the fight,
Fountain of mercy! acknowledge I Thee,
Father! oh bless Thou me!

Father! oh bless Thou me!
Into thy hands I my spirit commend.
My life Thou hast given, that life Thou canst end.
 For living, for dying, bless Thou me.
  Father! I worship Thee!

 Father, I worship Thee!
We strive not for gain or for earthly reward,
Our holiest rights we defend with our sword,
 Then, living and conquering, praise I Thee.
  Father! I trust in Thee!

 Father! I trust in Thee!
When all about me roll thunders of death,
Floweth my life-blood, and faileth my breath,
 Father in heaven! I trust still in Thee.
  Father! I call on Thee.

ADALBERT CHAMISSO DE BONCOURT.

[1781-1838.]

CASTLE BONCOURT.

I DREAM myself back to my childhood,
And shake my head agéd and grey;
How strangely ye haunt me, ye visions,
I deemed had long since passed away!

'Midst shady forests arising,
A stately castle behold;
I know the roof and the turrets,
The gate and the drawbridge old.

From out the armorial bearings,

The lions look down as of yore;

I greet those friends of my childhood,

And pass through the courtyard's door.

There lies the sphinx by the fountain,

There stands yet the fig-tree green:

My first young dream—I dreamed it

Behind yonder window's screen.

I enter the castle-chapel,

And seek my ancestor's grave;

'Tis there, there hangs from the pillar

The sword, and the banners wave.

I read not the tomb's inscription,

For tears have darkened my gaze,

Although through the painted windows
The sunlight joyously plays.

Thus wilt thou, oh, home of my fathers!
For aye in my memory last;
And thou from the earth hast vanished,
The plough has over thee passed.

I bless thee, oh, soil beloved!
I bless thee tenderly now,
And bless him doubly whoever
Guides o'er thy furrows the plough.

But I will again arouse me,
And with my harp in my hand,
Afar o'er the earth I'll wander,
And sing in many a land.

THE LION BRIDE.

WITH the bridal veil and the wreath in her hair,
The keeper's daughter, the maiden fair,
Comes into the den of the lion, to greet
The lion crouched at his mistress' feet.

The mighty brute, erst so fierce and wild,
Now gazes up to her meek and mild;
The lovely maiden, with mournful smile,
Caresses him softly, and weeps the while.

'We two were, in days long passed away,
Right faithful comrades at childish play:
No fonder playmates than thou and I—
The days of my childhood are now gone by.

'Around thy head—how, we scarcely knew—
Thy mane in its royal splendour grew;

I, too, am changed; thou see'st no more
Am I the child that I was before.

Oh, would that I still a child could be,
My fond and faithful old friend, with thee!
But I must go, though I willed it not,
To share, 'midst strangers, the stranger's lot.

' He praised my fairness, I know not why;
He wooed and won me, the hour is nigh;
The bridal wreath on my tresses lies,
And tears, fast gathering, dim my eyes.

' Dost hear me? thou lookest with angry brow;
Nay, see, I am tranquil; be calmer thou.
I see him coming, who waits for me—
Thus, friend, my last kiss I must give to thee.'

And as her farewell the maiden took,
The bars of iron they quivered and shook;
And when near the den he the youth espied,
Great terror seized on the trembling bride.

He takes his stand by the prison door,
With sweeping tail and with hideous roar;
She, praying, entreating, and threat'ning, demands
To go; unmoved, he angrily stands.

Without, confusion and shouts arise;
'Bring weapons, hasten!' the bridegroom cries;
'My hand is steady, my aim is good.'
Up springs the lion in savage mood.

The hapless bride dares to approach the door,
Then he falls on her he so loved before:

The beautiful form, a horrible prey,
Lies bloody and mangled,—a senseless clay.

And thus, the blood of his dearest shed,
He crouches grimly beside the dead.
He lies all lost in his sorrow and pain,
Till the bullet pierces his heart in twain.

LUDWIG UHLAND.
[1787-1862.]

THE MINSTREL'S CURSE.

THERE stood, in bygone ages, a castle old and grand,
It looked o'er vale and mountain, it looked o'er sea
    and land,
And sweetly-fragrant gardens lay blossoming around,
And rainbow-coloured fountains watered the turfy
    ground.

There dwelt a haughty monarch, with lands and
    treasures great;
He sat, so pale and gloomy, upon his throne of state.

His ev'ry word was terror, and death his ev'ry thought,
And blood and dire oppression he on his people brought.

Once came into this castle a noble minstrel pair—
The one with snow-white tresses, his son with golden hair.
The sire rode a palfrey sure, his harp behind him slung;
Beside him wandered gaily his comrade, blithe and young.

Then spake the aged minstrel: 'My son, I pray thee hear,
Sing all thy sweetest ditties in tones most full and clear;

To waken joy and sorrow unite thine ev'ry art,
To-day I fain would soften the monarch's iron heart.'

The minstrels were admitted into the marble hall,
There sat the haughty monarch, his queen and courtiers all—
The king in fearful splendour, like bloody northern light ;
The queen so sweet and gentle, like moonbeams through the night.

The aged minstrel touched his harp, its tones were wondrous clear,
And fuller still and fuller they struck the list'ning ear.
The youth's sweet voice melodiously rang forth in heavenly strain,
Anon the old man's deeper tones broke on the air again.

They sang of love and springtime, of golden days of
youth,
Of freedom, knightly doings, of holiness and truth :
They sang of all that winneth from mortal breast a sigh,
They sang of all that lifteth the mortal heart on high.

The fawning flattering courtiers forgot each mocking
word,
The king's rough, careless soldiers bowed down before
the Lord.
The queen she wept, she knew not if for sorrow or
for joy;
She flung the rosebud from her breast unto the
minstrel boy.

'Ye have allured my people, my queen ye seek
for now,'
The monarch cried in anger, with passion-clouded brow;

He flung his sword that through the breast of that
    young minstrel sped :
Instead of golden ditties, forth sprang a stream
    blood-red.

As though by storm-winds scattered, the hearers fled
    away,
A corpse within his master's arms, the fair boy-
    minstrel lay.
He wrapped his mantle o'er him, and bound him firm
    and fast
Upon his horse in silence, and from the hall he passed.

But ere he left the castle he halted at the door,
And seized his harp, more precious than e'er was harp
    before ;

Upon a marble pillar that much-loved harp he broke,

Then in a weird and thrilling tone these fatal words he spoke :—

'Woe to thee, stately castle ; woe to you, lofty halls !

No more the minstrel's harp and song shall echo through your walls ;

No ! only sighs and moanings, and slaves' sad footsteps hush'd,

Until the spirit of revenge has ground you into dust.

Woe to you, blooming gardens, all bathed in sunny light ;

Look, look upon this death-cold face, and shudder at the sight :

That sealed be every fountain, that ev'ry flower may die,
And that in after years these lands may bare and stony lie.

'Woe to thee, hated murd'rer, who bear'st a monarch's name,
In vain shall be thy striving for wreaths of bloody fame;
Thy name shall be forgotten, of thee no bard shall sing
In after years, no one shall know thou wast a mighty king.'

The minstrel's words were spoken, the Lord from heaven heard;
The castle lies in ruins, fulfilling thus His word.

Only one marble pillar tells of that lofty hall;
E'en this, already crumbling, before the night may fall.

The garden's now a desert, all stony, rough, and bare;
No tree gives grateful shelter, no flowers perfume the air;
The monarch's name no chronicle records, or minstrel's verse,
For evermore forgotten! Such was the Minstrel's Curse.

THE HOSTESS' DAUGHTER.

Three youths crossed over the river Rhine,
In an ancient tavern they called for wine:
' Hast, hostess, yet of thy wine so rare?
What does thy daughter, that maiden fair?'

'My ale is cool, my wine is clear,

My daughter lies on her sable bier.'

And when they came to the chamber, there

She lay on her bier, that maiden fair.

The eldest the flowing veil did raise,

And looked upon her with mournful gaze.

'Oh! wert thou still living, thou fairest on earth,

I would love thee truly from this day forth!'

The second drew down the veil again,

And turned him away, and wept with pain.

'Alas! that thou art on thy sable bier!

I have loved thee truly for many a year!'

The youngest threw back the sable veil,

And kissed her fair lips, so cold and so pale:

'I love thee to-day, as I loved thee before,

And I will love thee for evermore.'

FAITHFUL WALTER.

The faithful Walter riding near
Our Lady's chapel holy,
Beheld a maid in penitence
Before the threshold lowly :
' Oh, Walter, stay ! forsake me not !
Hast thou so soon the voice forgot
Thou erst didst hear with pleasure ? '

' Whom see I here ? the maiden false,
Whom once I called my own.
Where didst thou leave thy silken garb,
Where gold and precious stone ? '
' Woe ! that I did my faith betray !
My paradise I cast away ;
With thee again I find it.'

He raised to horse that lovely form,

He felt compassion tender,

And close about his neck she wound

Her arms so white and slender.

'Oh, Walter mine! my heart that beats

So warmly, nought but iron meets;

Alas! on thine it beats not.'

To Walter's castle then they came,

Whence life and joy were banished.

He took the helmet from his brow,

His youthful bloom had vanished:

'Thine eyes so dim, thy cheeks so worn,

My faithful love, thee best adorn;

I ne'er so fair beheld thee.'

The armour now unclasps the maid

For him whom she offended.

'Alas! a sable garb I see -
Thy love in death has ended.'
'My true-love I am mourning sore,
Whom I on earth shall never more
Nor yet in heaven recover.'

Now at his feet the maiden sinks,
With arms uplifted, sighing:
'A penitent behold me here,
To thee for mercy crying:
Oh! let me once again be blest,
Oh! let me on thy faithful breast
Be healed from ev'ry sorrow!'

'Arise, arise, unhappy child!
I can uplift thee never;

Mine arms too closely folded are,

My breast is lifeless ever.

Mourn thou, as I do, evermore,

For love is o'er, for love is o'er,

And ne'er again returneth.'

DREAM.

Within a garden shady

Two lovers hand in hand,

Wan knight and pallid lady,

They sat in the flowery land.

They kissed each other's faces,

Their lips with kisses burned;

Close, close were their embraces,

And youth and strength returned.

Two bells resounded shrilly,
The dream that instant fled:
She lay in convent stilly,
He in a dungeon dread.

THE SERENADE.

'WHAT strains of music sweet and clear
Rouse me from slumber deep?
Oh, mother! see who it may be,
Now all around doth sleep.'

'Nothing I hear, I nothing see,
Oh slumber soft again!
No love-songs now are sung to thee,
Left fading in thy pain.'

'It is no earthly melody
Fills me with joy so bright;
Angels are calling me with song:
O mother dear, good-night.'

J. O. L.

THE SHEPHERD'S SABBATH SONG.

It is the Sabbath-day,
Alone upon the plain I stand;
One matin-bell rings o'er the land,
Then silence holdeth sway.

I pray on bended knee,
Oh terror sweet! oh secret fear!
As though unseen were many here
To kneel and pray with me.

The heavens ev'ry way,

In such a holy quiet lie,

As though their op'ning must be nigh:

This is the Sabbath-day.

PARTING.

WHAT ringeth and singeth adown the street?

Come, open your windows, ye maidens sweet!

A youth leaves the town to-day,

His comrades they show him the way.

The others in mirth fling their caps in the air,

All decked with ribbons and flowers fair;

But the youth he loves not the revels gay,

And pale and silent goes on his way.

The goblets are ringing, high sparkles the wine,

'Drink once and again, dearest brother of mine,

With the parting cup can but flee

What burneth and gloweth in me.'

And there at the last house of all the street,

Looked out of her window a maiden sweet;

She sought to hide that her eyes were wet,

Behind the roses and mignonette.

And there, at the last house of all the street,

The youth looked up with a gesture fleet,

And sadly looked down again,

His hand on his heart as in pain.

'Dear brother, and hast thou no posy fair?

Full many a flower is blossoming there.'

'Arise! thou fairest of all,

And quickly a posy let fall.'

'Dear brothers, what use were the posy to me?

I have no true-love, so fair to see;

It would fade in the sun's burning ray,

And the wind would bear it away.'

And farther and farther, with cheer and song,

And the maiden listens, and listens long.

'Alas that the youth must depart,

Whom I loved in my secret heart!

'And here I stand with this love of mine,

With mignonette and with roses fine,

And he on whom I'd all bestow

So gladly, far from me must go.'

FRIEDERICH RÜCKERT.

[1789 - 1866.]

BARBAROSSA.

The mighty Barbarossa,
The Emp'ror Frederick old,
In subterranean chambers
Enchantments closely hold.

He never yet did perish,
He liveth there to-day,
And hidden in the castle,
He sits and sleeps away.

And he has taken with him
The splendour of his reign,
And at the time appointed
He will return again.

The Emperor is sitting
Upon an ivory chair;
His head upon a table
He leans, of marble rare.

His beard it is not flaxen,
It is of fiery glow,
And groweth through the table
On which his head lies low.

As though in dreams, he noddeth,
With scarce half-opened eyes,

And after long, long silence,

Unto a boy he cries.

In sleep to him he calleth,

'Look, dwarf, without the door,

If round the tower the ravens

Are flying as before.

'And if the ancient ravens

Around the tower still fly,

Yet hundred years, enchanted,

I here must sleeping lie.'

JUSTINUS KERNER.

[1786-1862.]

THE DYING MILLER.

THE stars shine o'er the vale below,
The mill-wheel turneth free;
I to the dying miller go,
He longs his friend to see.

I heard, as down the steps I went,
The mill-wheel's muffled roar,
In which a bell's soft chime was blent;
The daily task is o'er.

I stood beside the miller's bed,

He lay without a sound;

His heart was still, his spirit fled,

And silence reigned around.

His loved ones wept, lamenting sore,

Cold was his heart, and still;

Fast flow the waters as before,

But silent stands the mill.

TO THE DRINKING-GLASS OF A DEPARTED FRIEND.

FAIR glass, now empty dost thou stand,

Glass which so oft he raised with glee;

The spider now on either hand

Has spun her dismal web round thee.

Now shalt thou once again be filled
With gold of German vines, moon-bright;
I gaze, with pious trembling thrilled,
Into thy depths of sacred light.

What in those holy depths I saw,
No words had made me comprehend;
But there I learnt, with pious awe,
That nought can sever friend from friend.

In this belief, oh glass of mine!
I empty thee in joyful mood;
The stars, reflected, brightly shine,
Thou goblet, in thy precious blood.

Across the vale the moonbeams pass,
And midnight rings its solemn knell,
And strangely through the empty glass
The sacred sounds, re-echoing, dwell.

WILHELM MÜLLER.
[1795-1827.]

SONG.

I'D cut it on the bark of all the trees,

I'd grave it on each pebble that she sees,

I'd sow it on each bed in letters gay

Of green, that might my secret soon betray.

I'd write it on each leaf of ev'ry tree;

Thine is my heart, and ever thine shall be!

I'd breathe it to the morning's gentle gale,

I'd whisper it through ev'ry quiet dale;

Oh, could it shine from ev'ry flower star,

Could perfume waft it her, from near and far!

Can ye turn nought but wheels, ye waters free?

Thine is my heart, and ever thine shall be!

I thought mine eyes must soon the secret show,

That on my cheeks it stood in burning glow,

That on my silent lips it must appear,

That ev'ry breath proclaimed it loud and clear.

And she will not my anxious longing see;

Thine is my heart, and ever thine shall be;

VINETA.

FROM the lowest depths of ocean welling,

Evening bells are ringing mournfully;

Wondrous tidings unto us they're telling,
Of the ancient city, fair and free.

In the lap of ocean lost for ever,
Deep below its ruins still appear;
Beams its spires emit, that gleam and quiver
When reflected on the surface clear.

And the boatman who th' enchanted sparkle
Once saw, in the sunset's crimson glow,
Rows there ever, when it 'gins to darkle,
Though the rocks around their summits show.

From the depths of mine own heart are welling
Sounds, like bells of evening mournfully;
Wondrous tidings unto me they're telling,
Of the love erst all so dear to me.

Fair and bright's the world there lost for ever,
Still its ruins deep below appear;
Showing heavenly rays that shining quiver,
In my dreams—strange mirror ever clear.

Fain I'd plunge into those depths unbounded,
Gladly sink in that reflected light;
Oft, meseems, that angel voices sounded,
Calling me to that old city bright.

HEINRICH HEINE.

[1800-1856.]

SONG.

On the wings of my song, belovéd,
I'll bear thee the wide world o'er,
To a spot of infinite beauty
On the mystical Ganges' shore.

A rose-red blossoming garden
Lies calm in the moonlight fair;
The lotus flowers are awaiting
Their own little sister there.

The violets merrily murmur,

And gaze at the starlit sky,

The roses whisper together

Sweet magic of days gone by.

Thither come softly to listen,

The innocent, wise gazelles,

And far through the night, the rushing

Of the sacred river swells.

There will we sink down together,

'Neath palm-trees beside the stream,

And drink of love and of quiet,

And dream a heavenly dream.

THE LOTUS FLOWER.

The lotus flower feareth
The sun's resplendent light,
And, on her stem reclining,
Awaits she, dreaming, the night.

The moon is her gentle lover,
He wakes her with radiance pale,
And she for him will gladly
Her flower-face unveil.

She blooms and glows and brightens,
And gazes mutely above;
She sheddeth tears and perfume,
With love and the passion of love.

SONG.

When I look into thine eyes,
All my woe and sorrow flies;
But when I press my lips on thine,
Youth and health once more are mine.

When I lean upon thy breast,
There steals o'er me a heav'nly rest;
But when thou say'st, 'I love but thee!'
Then must I weep, ah, bitterly!

J. O. L.

SONG.

I.

No wrath I bear, although my heart despair,
Oh! love for ever lost! no wrath I bear!

Howe'er thou shinest in thy diamond light,
There falls no ray into thy spirit's night.

I know it well. I saw thee erst in dreams,
And saw the night wherein no sunshine gleams,
And saw the serpent eating at thy heart,
And saw how wholly wretched, love, thou art!

II.

Yes! thou art wretched, and no wrath I bear;
'Tis fated, love, we both shall wretched be,
Till death shall end our love-sick hearts' despair;
'Tis fated, love, we both shall wretched be.

I see the scorn upon thy lips close pressed,
I see thine eyes with cold defiance shine,

I see the angry pride that fills thy breast,

And yet thy lot is wretched e'en as mine.

That mouth it quivers with its secret woes,

Those eyes are dim with tears that none may see,

That haughty breast a hidden anguish knows,

'Tis fated, love, we both must wretched be.

SONG.

AND did but the little flowers

How deeply thou woundest me know,

Their tears with mine in showers,

To heal my grief, would flow.

And if the nightingales found me

So weary and sad and ill,

They would the air around me
With joyous melody fill.

And if my sorrow unending
The golden stars could see,
They'd come from their heights, descending,
And whisper comfort to me.

They know not what still is unspoken,
One only my grief can divine,
And she it is who has broken,
Yes! broken this heart of mine.

ANOTHER.

Does not my pallid face to thee
Betray my true love sorrow,

And wouldst thou that this haughty mouth
A beggar's words should borrow?

Ah no! this mouth, too proud, could naught
But jests or kisses cherish;
'Twould speak perchance a scornful word,
While I for grief did perish.

THE WATER-LILY.

THE slender water-lily
Looks up from the lake below;
The moon looks down to greet her
With shining lover's woe.

Adown to the quiet waters
She bends in her coy disdain,
And there at her feet beholdeth
Her poor pale wooer again.

THE LURELEI.

I KNOW not wherefore is beating
My heart so sadly to-day,
And ever I go repeating
A mystical fairy lay.

The evening breezes are blowing,
The Rhine flows peacefully by,
The mountain summits are glowing
Beneath the sunset sky.

On highest rock reclineth
A maiden wondrous fair;
The gold of her raiment shineth,
She combeth her golden hair.

She combs it with comb all golden,

And sings the while a song,

That has a melody olden,

Enchanted, wondrously strong.

The fisher who hears it o'er him,

Such passionate yearnings thrill,

He sees not the rocks before him,

But upwards he gazes still.

I fear me the waves will devour

The boat and the fisher ere long,

And this has been wrought by the power

Of the Lurelei's magic song.

WE SAT IN A LITTLE BOAT, LOVE.

WE sat in a little boat, love,
Together side by side;
And through the night did float, love,
Over the waters wide.

The spirit-island so fair, love,
In moonlight glimmering hung;
Sweet songs resounded there, love,
The mist-dance swayed and swung.

'Twas sweet, and yet more sweet, love,
And still swayed to and fro,
But we o'er the waters fleet, love,
Drifted in hopeless woe.

I SEE THEE OFT IN DREAMS AGAIN.

I SEE thee oft in dreams again,
And see thee greet me kindly;
And weeping loudly, I cast me then
Before thy sweet feet blindly.

Thou gazest at me mournfully,
Thy golden tresses shaking,
And from thy gentle eyes I see
The pearly tear-drops breaking.

Thou giv'st me a branch of the cypress drear,
One word thou whisperest, lowly:
I wake—the branch is no longer here,
And the word I've forgotten wholly.

I DREAMED.

I DREAMÉD of a royal maid,
So tearful, pale, and slender,
We sat beneath the lime-tree, clasped
In love's embraces tender.

'I would not have thy father's throne,
His crown of diamonds rarest;
I would not have his sceptre's state,
But thee thyself, thou fairest.'

'That cannot be,' she answered then,
'For in my grave I'm lying;
And only at night I come to thee,
Because of my love undying.'

SONG.

I STOOD and leant against the mast,
Counted each wavelet's swell;
The ship it sails so fast, too fast;
Dear Fatherland, farewell!

My fair-love's house I glide before,
Her casements catch the sun,
With gazing long my eyes are sore,
But greeting waves me none.

Ye welling tears, keep from mine eyes,
Lest I in darkness go;
And break not thou, my weary heart,
With all too bitter woe!

                                    J. O L.

HOFFMANN von FALLERSLEBEN.

[1798-   .]

PARTING.

The flowers that the lea adorn,
The grass all wet with dew of morn,
The tree that garb of green doth show,
   All cry, ' Farewell, I go!
     Farewell, I go!'

The roses with their petals bright,
The lilies robed like angels white,
The blossoms on the heath that glow—
   All cry, ' Farewell, I go!
     Farewell, I go!'

'Tis coming all, and going fleet,

A parting and a meeting sweet;

We pass through joy and hope and woe,

Then far apart must go,

Farewell! we go.

And we had scarcely met once more,

When like a fair dream all was o'er;

Then clasped we hands and whispered low,

'Farewell, farewell, I go,

Farewell! I go.'

CRADLE SONG.

ALL is wrapped in slumber mild,

Sleep thou also, sleep, my child!

Through the trees the night-winds sweep,

Soft and low! my darling, sleep!

Close thine eyes, so dear to me,
That they like two buds may be;
When the sun at morn doth glow,
They will, like the flowers, blow.

And the flowers there I see,
Kiss the eyes so dear to me;
And the mother thinks no more
That 'tis spring without the door.

J. C. FREIHERR von ZEDLITZ.
[1790-1862.]

THE ROBBER'S WIFE.

THE sun is setting so luridly red,
As though my true-love were prisoned and dead;
They have come down from the rocky hill,
They watch in the vale, they wait by the hill.

They crouch in ditches and brushwood high,
Between the ruined old walls they lie;
And the road is held, and the pass is manned,
And on yonder height the sentinels stand.

Oh! sleep, my baby; my little one, sleep,
In the shady grot, by the fountain deep,
And a dainty lullaby I will sing
Of the nightly dance in the elfin ring.

'Ye elves, come, weave me'—What is't I hear?
A shot! 'Twas his followers' greeting cheer;
And he who receives it, his cares are o'er;
He sleeps in peace, and awakes no more.

'Ye elves, come, weave me your floating veil'—
Hark! shot on shot ringing through the dale;
Up whirls the smoke, with its clouds blue-grey;
Ah! why is the combat so fierce to-day?

'Ye elves, come, weave me your floating veil,
For my darling child in your moonlit dale'—

That was his musket, its sound I hear,
None other thunders so loud and clear.

And shot upon shot—no travellers they,
The servants of justice seize their prey;
No thought of booty is in that strife;
Alas! they are venturing life for life.

Ah, woe is me! How cold is my brow!
My true-love's shots, they are silent now;
I hear them no more—his musket is hushed;
Oh! how the blood to my heart it rushed!

My knees are trembling! Ah! woe is me!
My child, let us hasten, hasten to flee;
The sun is setting so luridly red,
As though my true-love were lying dead.

NICOLAUS LENAU.
[1802 - 1850.]

THE GIPSIES.

THREE gipsy men I once did see
Beneath a tree together,
As my waggon wearily
Crept o'er sandy heather.

And his fiddle one did hold,
From his comrades straying,
In the glowing sunset's gold
Fiery ditties playing.

And his pipe the second bore,
Watched the smoke that speeded
Free, as though on earth no more
He for gladness needed.

And, his lute hung on a tree,
Lay the third one sleeping;
O'er the string the breezes free,
Dreams his heart o'ersweeping.

Rents did all their garments show,
Gaily hued and tattered,
Yet they faced the world as though
Fortune little mattered.

Threefold thus of life did they
Show how light we prize it,

Fiddle, smoke, and sleep all day,

And three times despise it.

Many a time I gazed around

At those three together,

At those faces deeply browned,

And locks like raven's feather.

SEDGE SONG.

MOONLIGHT calm and still reposes

On the waveless lake beneath,

Weaving all its pallid roses

In the sedges' verdant wreath.

Deer upon the hill-side yonder,

Out into the darkness gaze,

Dreamily the wild-fowl wander,

Rustling through the reedy maze.

Tears my downcast eyes are filling,

In my deepest soul I bear

Thoughts of thee, my spirit thrilling

Like a silent midnight prayer.

ANNETTE von DROSTE HÜLFSHOF.

[1798-1848.]

THE MERCHANT'S WIFE.

A CERTAIN merchant had a wife,

He deemed was nigh too soft and mild,

Too gentle for this daily life;

Too like the moonbeams when she smiled,

As through the house he watched her go,

All shadow-like with noiseless tread.

He strove, as with an unseen foe,

Too keep an angry word unsaid.

But more than all did him provoke

One saying that she used with all,

Of grave or gay, whate'er she spoke,

Her lips, unthinkingly, let fall:

'In Heaven's name,' she softly said,

When times of grief or trial came,

And when her husband drank or played,

Again she said, 'In Heaven's name.'

He thought it foolish, even wrong,

Nay, taking Heaven's name in vain;

He scolds, she weeps; but still ere long

Forgets it o'er and o'er again.

It was a habit learnt within

The convent, where she spent her youth;

And thus it was no special sin,

Nor any special good, in truth!

The proverb says, Whose cup runs o'er
With joy, frets at the buzzing fly;
And thus this saying vexed him more
Than others' lies and treachery.
And if she owned her fault, and sought
His anger meekly to assuage,
He swore that, whatsoe'er she thought,
It would arouse his shame and rage.

But he who seeks distress and need,
Will meet them on his way at length;
Oft commerce proves a fragile reed,
Depending much on others' strength.
A friend has failed, a debtor flees,
A creditor no more will wait,
And ere the year is out, it sees
Debt standing at our merchant's gate.

His wife had marked him wand'ring by,

All lost in thought, with care oppressed,

Or in his office sit and sigh;

And so at last, his secret guessed,

Unto her hidden store she sped,

Took something from her cupboard's 'gloom,

Then shadow-like, with noiseless tread,

She glided to her husband's room.

He sat, his hand upon his brow,

With pipe unlit and visage drear:

' Karl,' came a noiseless whisper now

And then again upon his ear.

She stood before him all aglow,

As though some failing to confess:

' Karl, trouble threatens us, I know;

Is there no means to make it less?'

Then closer to his side she stept,

Upon his knee a bag to lay;

Her little treasure there she kept

Her savings for a needy day.

He cast at her a rapid glance,

And counted it with vain desire,

Then sighing said, ' My evil chance

Would twice as much as this require.'

A paper in his hand she laid,

Then turned away with heaving breast;

It was a little income paid

To her by some old aunt's bequest.

' Nay, nay,' he said, 'that must not be,'

And stroked her cheek of burning glow,

Then looking at it eagerly,

' 'Tis nigh enough,' he muttered low.

Her little treasures then she drew

From out her apron's snowy fold :

Some ancient trinkets, tea-spoons new,

A string of ducats bent and old :

She gave it with such joy, and yet

Around her mouth a quiver passed,

As by the motley heap, she set

Her mother's wedding-ring at last.

' 'Tis nigh enough,' her husband said,

' Yet may the end fulfil my fears ;

But canst thou bear to earn thy bread

In poverty through coming years ? '

She looked at him ! ah, none can know

But love, thus on love's gaze to dwell :

' In Heaven's name,' she whispered low ;

And, weeping, on her neck he fell.

ANASTASIUS GRÜN.

[1806-   .]

MANHOOD'S TEAR.

MAIDEN, saw'st thou erst me weeping?
Mark, a woman's tear I deem
Like the heavenly dews, that brightly
In the flower's chalice gleam.

If at midnight's gloomy hour,
Or 'neath morning's cheerful skies,
Still the dew-drops bid the flower
All refreshed again arise.

But a man's tear most resembles
That rich sap the orient knows;
Hidden in the tree, but rarely
Of its own free will it flows.

Thou must cleave the bark, and pierce it
To the inmost heart of all,
Perfect, pure, and clear, and golden,
Then the precious drops will fall.

Soon indeed their flowing ceases,
And the tree grows green again;
Many a spring-time will it welcome,
But the wound, the scar remain.

Maid, the wounded tree, remember,
On the distant orient steep;
And the man remember, maiden,
Whom thou late beheldest weep.

ERNST von FEUCHTERSLEBEN.

[1806 - 1849.]

IT IS ALMIGHTY GOD'S DECREE.

It is Almighty God's decree
That from our dearest there must be
    A parting,
Although there's nought on earth below
That causes us such bitter woe
    As parting.

If one gives thee a rosebud rare,
In water set the flow'ret fair;
    But know

That if a rose bloom forth next day,
Before the night 'twill fade away—
　　This know.

And if God gives a love to thee,
Thou holdest her thine own to be
　　To keep,
She'll be but little while thine own,
Then she will leave thee quite alone—
　　Then weep.

But thou must understand me well:
When parting friends their sorrows tell,
　　They say,
'Until we meet, farewell!'

WILHELM WACKERNAGEL.

[1806-1869.]

THE WEEPING WILLOW.

I, LIKE the willow, put forth leaf,
The willow weeping;
Who raiseth not her head in grief,
Her lone watch keeping.

She stands, and weeps, and lets adown
Her long hair flow,
Where fragrant flowers o'er a grave
And grasses grow.

To her e'en spring of swelling buds

Hath brought his dole :

When will the green leaf fade and fall,

Reaching its goal?

J. O. L.

EMANUEL GEIBEL.
[1815-   .]

FROM AFAR.

Say, wild heart, torn by passion's bitter throe,
What meaneth now this throbbing fiery fast?
Wilt thou, after such weary, nameless woe,
    Not rest at last?

Thy youth has passed away, its perfume fled;
With it the heaven that once thine own did seem;
The tree of life its rosy bloom hath shed—
    'Twas all a dream!

The blossom fell, but mine remains the thorn;
Still, still the crimson stream the wound doth lave;
The woe, the passionate longing, and the scorn,
    Are all I have.

And yet didst Lethe's waters to me bring,
And say, Thou shalt be healed; drink, then, and know
Forgetfulness, how wondrous sweet a thing!
    I'd say: Not so.

E'en though 'twas but a vision swift to pass,
Its blissful sweetness seemed of heaven above;
Too well with ev'ry breath I know, alas!
    That still I love.

Then let me go; my bleeding heart I'd fain
Bear to some quiet spot, where night and day
In my last song I all my love and pain
    May breathe away.

J. O. L.

THE WANDERING SPANIARD.

Southern Spain, the land of beauty,
Spain is my own fatherland,
Where the chestnuts tall and shady
Rustle on the Ebro's strand.
Where the rosy almond blossoms,
Where the vine in purple glows,
Where the moonlight gleams more brightly,
And more lovely seems the rose.

Now I with my lute must wander
Sadly forth from door to door,
But no kind, bright eyes are looking
Out upon me as of yore.
Scarce and scanty alms they give me,
Coldly then they bid me go;
Ah! the poor brown Spanish wand'rer
None will understand or know.

How this mist weighs down upon me,

Distancing the sun's bright ray!

How have all my merry ditties

From my mem'ry passed away!

Still, whatever be the music,

One sad note is ever there;

I would seek my own dear country,

Land of sunshine bright and fair.

When last harvest-time, the village

Held a joyous holiday,

Of my songs, to aid the dancing,

I the very best did play.

But when all were dancing gaily

In the sunset's evening gold,

O'er my brown cheeks slowly, sadly,

Hot and fast, the tear-drops rolled.

Ah! I thought amidst the gladness
Of some balmy Spanish night,
When beneath the fragrant moonbeams
Ev'ry heart becomes more light;
When unto the zither's measure
Eager feet with swiftness hie,
And the youth and maiden, glowing,
Through the wild fandango fly.

No! my heart's unbounded yearning
I no longer can restrain;
Be all other joys denied me,
Give me but my home again.
Hence to Spain, the land of beauty,
Land of sunshine bright and fair,
In the shadow of the chestnuts,
Oh! I must be buried there!

MY HEART IS LIKE THE GLOOMY NIGHT.

My heart is like the gloomy night,
    When all the tree-tops shiver ;
Forth breaks the moon in splendour bright,
    From clouds so light—
And see ! the list'ning wood has ne'er a quiver.

The moon, the radiant moon thou art
    Of all thy rich love's treasure,
Let one glance only be my part ;
    And see ! this heart
In heavenly peace hath lost its stormy measure.

J. O. L.

GOTTFRIED KINKEL.

[1815-   .]

EVENING HYMN.

It is so calm and silent,

The evening winds are still,

And angel footsteps softly

Are heard on ev'ry hill.

    Now sinks upon the valley

    The darkness far and near;

    Oh, heart! forget thy sorrow,

    And cast aside thy fear.

The world now rests in silence,

Its tumult is gone by,

Hushed are the songs of gladness,

And hushed is sorrow's cry.

 If roses were thy portion,

 If thorns or petals sere,

 Oh, heart! forget thy sorrow,

 And cast aside thy fear.

And though thy sins be many,

Oh! look not back to-night,

But feel thyself inspired

By mercy's free delight.

 On high the Shepherd watcheth

 His erring children here;

 Oh, heart! forget thy sorrow,

 And cast aside thy fear.

Now in the heaven's circle

The stars in splendour rise,

In firm and even motion

The golden chariot hies.

 And like the stars, He guideth

 Thy way through midnight drear.

 Oh, heart! forget thy sorrow,

 And cast aside thy fear.

THE END.

COLSTON AND SON, PRINTERS, EDINBURGH.

A SELECTION FROM

HENRY S. KING & CO.'S

LIST OF NEW BOOKS.

65, *Cornhill, and* 1, *Paternoster Square,*

May, 1876.

A SELECTION

FROM

HENRY S. KING AND CO.'S CATALOGUE.

NEW AND RECENTLY PUBLISHED WORKS.

CHILDREN'S BOOKS.

THREE SHILLINGS AND SIXPENCE EACH.

Works by the Author of "St. Olave's," "When I was a Little Girl," &c.

UNT MARY'S BRAN PIE. Illustrated. Foolscap 8vo, cloth.

Sunnyland Stories. Illustrated. Foolscap 8vo, cloth.

Brave Men's Footsteps : a Book of Example and Anecdote for Young People. By the Editor of "Men who have Risen." With 4 Illustrations by C. Doyle. Third Edition. Crown 8vo cloth.

Pretty Lessons in Verse for Good Children, with some Lessons in Latin, in easy Rhyme. By SARA COLERIDGE. Illustrated. A New Edition. Foolscap 8vo, cloth.

Little Minnie's Troubles : an Every-Day Chronicle. By N. D'ANVERS. Illustrated by W. H. Hughes. Foolscap 8vo., cloth.

The Desert Pastor, Jean Jarousseau. By Colonel E. P. DE L'HOSTE. Translated from the French of Eugène Pelletan. With an Engraved Frontispiece. New Edition. Fcap. 8vo, cloth.

The Story of Our Father's Love, told to Children, being a New and Enlarged Edition of THEOLOGY FOR CHILDREN. By MARK EVANS. Foolscap 8vo, cloth.

Works by MARTHA FARQUHARSON.

Elsie Dinsmore. Illustrated, Foolscap 8vo, cloth.

Elsie's Girlhood. Illustrated, Foolscap 8vo, cloth.

Elsie's Holiday at Roselands. Illustrated, Fcap. 8vo, cloth.

The Little Wonder-Horn. A Second Series of "Stories told to a Child." By JEAN INGELOW. With Fifteen Illustrations. Square 24mo, cloth.

Plucky Fellows. A Book for Boys. By STEPHEN J. MACKENNA. With Six Illustrations. Second Edition. Crown 8vo, cloth.

The African Cruiser. A Midshipman's Adventures on the West Coast. By S. W. SADLER, R.N., Author of "Marshall Vavasour." A Book for Boys. With Three Illustrations. Third Edition. Crown 8vo, cloth.

Seeking His Fortune, and Other Stories. With 4 Illustrations. Crown 8vo, cloth.

Seven Autumn Leaves from Fairyland. Illustrated with Nine Etchings. Square 8vo, cloth.

Works by SARA COLERIDGE.

Pretty Lessons in Verse for Good Children, with some Lessons in Latin, in Easy Rhyme. A New Edition. Illustrated. Foolscap 8vo, cloth.

Phantasmion. A Fairy Romance. With an Introductory Preface by the Right Hon. Lord Coleridge of Ottery St. Mary. A New Edition. Illustrated. Crown 8vo, cloth, price 7s. 6d.

FIVE SHILLINGS EACH.

Works by JAMES BONWICK.

The Tasmanian Lily. With Frontispiece. Crown 8vo, cloth.

Mike Howe, the Bushranger of Van Diemen's Land. With Frontispiece. Crown 8vo, cloth.

Rambles and Adventures of Our School Field Club: its Adventures and Achievements. A Book for Boys. By G. C. DAVIES. Crown 8vo, cloth.

Works by DAVID KER.

The Boy Slave in Bokhara: a Tale of Central Asia. With Illustrations. Crown 8vo, cloth.

The Wild Horseman of the Pampas. Illustrated. Crown 8vo, cloth.

Fantastic Stories. By RICHARD LEANDER. Translated from the German by PAULINA B. GRANVILLE. With 8 Full-page Illustrations by M. E. Fraser-Tytler. Crown 8vo, cloth.

Her Title of Honour: a Book for Girls. By HOLME LEE. New Edition, with Frontispiece. Crown 8vo, cloth.

At School with an Old Dragoon. By STEPHEN J. MACKENNA. With 6 Illustrations. Crown 8vo, cloth.

Slavonic Fairy Tales. From Russian, Servian, Polish, and Bohemian Sources. By JOHN T. NAAKÉ, of the British Museum. With 4 Illustrations. Crown 8vo, cloth.

Waking and Working; or, from Girlhood to Womanhood. By Mrs. G. S. REANEY. With Frontispiece. Crown 8vo, cloth.

Stories in Precious Stones. By HELEN ZIMMERN. With 6 Illustrations. Third Edition. Crown 8vo, cloth.

Works by Miss M. BETHAM-EDWARDS.

Kitty. With a Frontispiece. Crown 8vo, cloth, price 3s. 6d.

Mademoiselle Josephine's Fridays, and Other Stories. Crown 8vo, cloth, price 7s. 6d.

By Still Waters. A Story for Quiet Hours. By EDWARD GARRETT. With Seven Illustrations. Crown 8vo, cloth, price 6s.

Works by Mrs. G. S. REANEY.

Waking and Working; or, from Girlhood to Womanhood. With a Frontispiece. Crown 8vo, cloth, price 5s.

Sunbeam Willie, and other Stories, for Home Reading and Cottage Meetings. 3 Illustrations. Small square, uniform with "Lost Gip," &c. Cloth, price 1s. 6d.

Locked Out: a Tale of the Strike. By ELLEN BARLEE. With a Frontispiece. Cloth, price 1s. 6d.

Daddy's Pet. A Sketch from Humble Life. By Mrs. ELLEN ROSS, ("Nelsie Brook.") With 6 Illustrations. Square crown 8vo. Uniform with "Lost Gip." Cloth, price 1s.

Works by the Author of "Jessica's First Prayer," (HESBA STRETTON).

The Wonderful Life. With Illustrated Frontispiece. Fcap. 8vo, cloth, price 2s. 6d. Ninth Thousand.

With Illustrations, square crown 8vo, cloth, price 1s. 6d. each.

The Crew of the Dolphin.

Cassy. Twenty-seventh thousand.

Lost Gip. Forty-sixth thousand.

The King's Servants. Thirty-third thousand.

Also a handsomely-bound Edition, with 12 Illustrations, price 2s. 6d.

PRICE SIXPENCE EACH.

With Frontispiece, Small Square, Limp Cloth.

Friends till Death.	**Two Christmas Stories.**
Old Transome.	**Michel Lorio's Cross.**

The Worth of a Baby, and **How Apple Tree Court was Won.**

POETRY.

ALLADS OF GOOD DEEDS, AND OTHER
Verses. By HENRY ABBEY. Foolscap 8vo, cloth, gilt, price 5s.

Lyrics of Love, from Shakespeare to Tennyson. Selected and arranged by W. DAVENPORT ADAMS, Jun. Foolscap 8vo, cloth extra, gilt edges, price 3s. 6d.

Through Storm and Sunshine. By ADON. Illustrated by M. E. Edwards, A. T. H. Paterson, and the Author. Crown 8vo., cloth, price 7s. 6d.

Pindar in English Rhyme. Being an attempt to render the Epinikian Odes with the principal remaining Fragments of Pindar, into English Rhymed Verse. By T. C. BARING, M.P., late Fellow of Brasenose College, Oxford. Small quarto, cloth, price 7s.

Home Songs for Quiet Hours. By the Rev. Canon R. H. BAYNES, Editor of "Lyra Anglicana," &c. Second Edition. Foolscap 8vo, cloth extra, price 3s. 6d.

This may also be had handsomely bound in Morocco with gilt edges.

Metrical Translations from the Greek and Latin Poets, and other Poems. By R. B. BOSWELL, M.A., Oxon. Crown 8vo cloth, price 5s.

Poems. By WILLIAM CULLEN BRYANT. Red-line Edition, With 24 Illustrations and Portrait of the Author. Square Crown 8vo, cloth, price 7s. 6d.

A Cheaper Edition, with Frontispiece, cloth, price 3s. 6d.

Poems by Dr. W. C. BENNETT.

Songs for Sailors. Dedicated by Special Request to H.R.H. the Duke of Edinburgh. With Steel Portrait and Illustrations. Crown 8vo, cloth, price 3s. 6d.

An Edition in Illustrated Paper Covers, price 1s.

Baby May. Home Poems and Ballads. With Frontispiece. Cloth elegant, Crown 8vo, cloth, price 6s.

Baby May and Home Poems. Foolscap 8vo, sewed in Coloured Wrapper. Price 1s.

Narrative Poems and Ballads. Foolscap 8vo, sewed in Coloured Wrapper. Price 1s.

Poems by ROBERT BUCHANAN.

Poetical Works. Collected Edition, in 3 Vols., price 6s. each.
Vol. I.—"Ballads and Romances;" "Ballads and Poems of Life;" and a Portrait of the Author.
Vol. II.—"Ballads and Poems of Life;" "Allegories and Sonnets."
Vol. III.—"Cruiskeen Sonnets;" "Book of Orm;" "Political Mystics."

Walled in, and Other Poems. By the Rev. HENRY J. BULKELEY. Crown 8vo, cloth, price 5s.

Calderon's Dramas: The Wonder-Working Magician—Life is a Dream—The Purgatory of St. Patrick. Translated by Denis Florence McCarthy. Post 8vo, cloth, price 10s.

Narcissus and Other Poems. By E. CARPENTER. Fcap. 8vo, cloth, price 5s.

Pretty Lessons in Verse for Good Children, with some Lessons in Latin, in Easy Rhyme. By SARA COLERIDGE. A New Edition. Illustrated. Foolscap 8vo, cloth, price 3s. 6d.

Cosmos. A Poem. Foolscap 8vo, cloth, price 3s. 6d.

Subjects—Nature in the Past and in the Present—Man in the Past and in the Present—The Future.

Poems by AUBREY DE VERE.

Alexander the Great. A Dramatic Poem. Small crown 8vo, cloth, price 5s.

The Infant Bridal, and other Poems. A New and Enlarged Edition. Foolscap 8vo, cloth, price 7s. 6d.

The Legends of St. Patrick, and other Poems. Small Crown 8vo, cloth, price 5s.

English Sonnets. Collected and arranged by JOHN DENNIS. Foolscap 8vo, cloth, price 3s. 6d.

Vignettes in Rhyme and Vers de Societe. By AUSTIN DOBSON. Second Edition. Foolscap 8vo, cloth, price 5s.

Hymns and Verses. Original and Translated. By the Rev. HENRY DOWNTON, M.A. Small Crown 8vo, cloth, price 3s. 6d.

Minor Chords ; or, Songs for the Suffering : A Volume of Verse. By the Rev. BASIL EDWARDS. Foolscap 8vo, cloth, price 3s. 6d.; paper, price 2s. 6d.

The Epic of Hades. By a New Writer. Author of "Songs of Two Worlds." Foolscap 8vo, cloth, price 5s.

Eros Agonistes. Poems. By E.B.D. Foolscap 8vo, cloth, price 3s. 6d.

Hymns for the Church and Home. Selected and Edited by the Rev. W. FLEMING STEVENSON.

The Hymn Book consists of Three Parts :—I. For Public Worship.—II. For Family and Private Worship.—III. For Children.

Published in various forms and prices, the latter ranging from 8d. to 6s. Lists and full particulars will be furnished on application to the Publishers.

On Viol and Flute. By EDMUND W. GOSSE. With Title-page specially designed by William B. Scott. Crown 8vo, cloth, price 5s.

A Tale of the Sea, Sonnets, and other Poems. By JAMES HOWELL. Foolscap 8vo, cloth, price 5s.

B

MR. TENNYSON'S WORKS.

Queen Mary : a Drama. New Edition, price 6s.

Mr. Tennyson's Works. The Author's Edition.

Vol. I.—Early Poems and English Idylls, cloth, price 6s. ; Rox., 7s. 6d.
II.—Locksley Hall, Lucretius, & other Poems ,, 6s. ,, 7s. 6d.
III.—The Idylls of the King, complete ,, 7s. 6d. ,, 9s.
IV.—The Princess and Maud ,, 6s. ,, 7s. 6d.
V.—Enoch Arden and In Memoriam ,, 6s. ,, 7s. 6d.

Price 31s. 6d. cloth gilt, or 39s. half-morocco, Roxburgh style.

Mr. Tennyson's Works. The Cabinet Edition. In 10 Half-Crown Volumes, each with a Frontispiece. These Volumes may be had separately, or the Edition complete, in handsome ornamental case, price 28s.

CONTENTS.

Vol. I.—Early Poems. Illustrated with a Photographic Portrait of Mr. Alfred Tennyson.

II.—English Idylls, and other Poems. Containing an Engraving of Mr. Alfred Tennyson's Residence at Aldworth.

III.—Locksley Hall, and other Poems. With an Engraved Picture of Farringford.

IV.—Lucretius, and other Poems. Containing an Engraving of a Scene in the Garden at Swainston.

V.—Idylls of the King. With an Autotype of the Bust of Mr. Alfred Tennyson, by T. Woolner, R.A.

VI.—Idylls of the King. Illustrated, with an Engraved Portrait of "Elaine," from a Photographic Study by Julia M. Cameron.

VII.—Idylls of the King. Containing an Engraving of "Arthur," from a Photographic Study by Julia M. Cameron.

VIII.—The Princess. With an Engraved Frontispiece.

IX.—Maud and Enoch Arden. With a Picture of " Maud," taken from a Photographic Study by Julia M. Cameron.

X.—In Memoriam. With a Steel Engraving of Arthur H. Hallam, Engraved from a Picture in possession of the Author by J. C. Armitage.

Mr. Tennyson's Works. The Library Edition. This Edition is in 6 octavo Volumes, printed in large, clear old-faced type, with a Steel Engraved Portrait of the Author, each volume price 10s. 6d., or the set complete, £3 3s.

CONTENTS.

Vol. I.—Miscellaneous Poems.

II.—Miscellaneous Poems.

III.—Princess and other Poems.

IV.—In Memoriam and Maud.

V.—Idylls of the King.

VI.—Idylls of the King.

Mr. Tennyson's Works. The Miniature Edition. In 11 Volumes, pocket size, bound in imitation vellum, ornamented in gilt and gilt edges, in case, price 35s. This Edition can also be had in plain binding and case, price 31s. 6d.; gilt extra, 35s.

Mr. Tennyson's Works. The Original Editions. Green cloth lettered.

	s.	d.
Poems ... ... reduced from 9s. to	6	0
Maud and other Poems ... ... ,, ,, 5s. ,,	3	6
The Princess ... ... ,, ,, 5s. ,,	3	6
Idylls of the King ... ... ,, ,, 7s. ,,	5	0
The Holy Grail ... ... ,, ,, 7s. ,,	4	6
Gareth and Lynette ... ... ,, ,, 5s. ,,	3	0
Idylls of the King, collected ... ... ,, ,, 12s. ,,	6	0
Enoch Arden ... ... ,, ,, 6s. ,,	3	6
In Memoriam ... ... ,, ,, 6s. ,,	4	0

All the various editions of Mr. Tennyson's Works may also be had in elegant binding, calf, Morocco, or Russia.

Selections from the Works of Mr. Tennyson. Cloth, reduced from 5s. to 3s. 6d., or gilt extra, 4s.

Songs from the Works of Mr. Tennyson. Reduced from 5s. to 3s. 6d., gilt extra, 4s.

Penelope, and Other Poems. By ALLISON HUGHES.
Foolscap 8vo, cloth, price 4s. 6d.

Poems by Mrs. HAMILTON KING.

The Disciples. A New Poem. Second Edition, with some Notes. Crown 8vo, cloth, price 7s. 6d.

Aspromonte, and Other Poems. Second Edition. Foolscap 8vo, cloth, price 4s. 6d.

Poems. By ANNETTE F. C. KNIGHT. Foolscap 8vo, cloth, price 5s.

The Lady of Lipari. A Poem in Three Cantos. Foolscap 8vo, cloth, price 5s.

The Gallery of Pigeons, and other Poems. By THEOPHILE MARZIALS. Crown 8vo, cloth, price 4s. 6d.

The Olympian and Pythian Odes of Pindar. A New Translation in English Verse. By the Rev. F. D. MORICE, M.A., Fellow of Queen's College, Oxford. Crown 8vo, cloth, price 7s. 6d.

The Inner and Outer Life Poems. By the Rev. A. NORRIS, B.A. Foolscap 8vo, cloth, price 6s.

Göethe's Faust. A New Translation in Rime. By C. KEGAN PAUL. Crown 8vo, cloth, price 6s.

Timoleon. A Dramatic Poem. By JAMES RHOADES. Foolscap 8vo, cloth, price 5s.

The Dream and the Deed, and other Poems. By PATRICK SCOTT. Foolscap 8vo, cloth, price 5s.

Songs of Two Worlds. By a New Writer. First Series. Second Edition, Foolscap 8vo, cloth, price 5s.

Songs of Two Worlds. By a New Writer. Second Series. Second Edition, Foolscap 8vo, cloth, price 5s.

Songs of Two Worlds. By a New Writer. Third Series. Second Edition, Foolscap 8vo, cloth, price 5s.

Songs for Music. By Four Friends. Square crown 8vo, cloth, price 5s. Containing Songs by—

  Reginald A. Gatty. | Greville J. Chester.
  Stephen H. Gatty. | Juliana H. Ewing.

Monacella: a Legend of North Wales. A Poem. By AGNES STONEHEWER, Foolscap 8vo, cloth, price 3s. 6d.

Poems. By the Rev. J. W. AUGUSTUS TAYLOR, M.A. Foolscap 8vo, cloth, price 5s.

Poems by Sir HENRY TAYLOR.

Edwin the Fair and Isaac Comnenus. Foolscap 8vo, cloth, price 3s. 6d.

A Sicilian Summer and Other Poems. Foolscap 8vo, cloth, price 3s. 6d.

Philip Van Artevelde. A Dramatic Poem. Foolscap 8vo, cloth, price 5s.

Thoughts in Verse. Small crown 8vo, cloth, price 1s. 6d.

Hymns and Sacred Lyrics. By the Rev. GODFREY THRING, B.A. Foolscap 8vo, cloth, price 5s.

Arvan; or, the Story of the Sword. A Poem. By HERBERT TODD, M.A. Crown 8vo, cloth, price 7s. 6d.

Sonnets, Lyrics, and Translations. By the Rev. CHARLES TURNER. Crown 8vo, cloth, price 4s. 6d.

On the North Wind—Thistledown. A Volume of Poems. By the Hon. Mrs. WILLOUGHBY. Small Crown 8vo, cloth, price 7s. 6d.

FICTION.

THE CORNHILL LIBRARY OF FICTION. Crown 8vo, cloth, price 3s. 6d. each.

ALF-A-DOZEN DAUGHTERS. By J. MASTERMAN.

The House of Raby. By Mrs. G. HOOPER.

A Fight for Life. By MOY THOMAS.

Robin Gray. By CHARLES GIBBON.

Kitty. By Miss M. BETHAM-EDWARDS.

One of Two ; or the Left-Handed Bride. By J. HAIN FRISWELL.

Ready-Money Mortiboy. A Matter-of-Fact Story.

God's Providence House. By Mrs. G. L. BANKS.

For Lack of Gold. By CHARLES GIBBON.

Hirell. By JOHN SAUNDERS.

Abel Drake's Wife. By JOHN SAUNDERS.

Culmshire Folk. A Novel. By IGNOTUS. New and Cheaper Edition in 1 vol. Crown 8vo, price 6s.

Her Title of Honour. A Book for Girls. By HOLME LEE. New Edition, with a Frontispiece, Crown 8vo, cloth, price 5s.

Russian Romance. By ALEXANDER SERGUEVITCH POUSHKIN. Translated from the Tales of Belkin, &c. By Mrs. J. Buchan Telfer (*née* Mouravieff). Crown 8vo, cloth, price 7s. 6d.

Memoirs of Mrs. Lætitia Boothby. By WILLIAM CLARK RUSSELL. Crown 8vo, price 7s. 6d.

Works by KATHERINE SAUNDERS. Crown 8vo, price 6s. each.

Gideon's Rock, and other Stories.

Joan Merryweather, and other Stories.

Margaret and Elizabeth. A Story of the Sea.

Works by Col. MEADOWS TAYLOR, C.S.I., M.R.I.H. Crown 8vo, cloth, price 6s. each.

The Confessions of a Thug.

Tara : a Mahratta Tale.

The Romantic Annals of a Naval Family. By Mrs. ARTHUR TRAHERNE. A New and Cheaper Edition, crown 8vo, cloth, price 5s.

HISTORY AND TRAVEL.

THE HISTORY OF JAPAN. From the Earliest Period to the Present Time. By F. O. ADAMS, H.B.M.'s Secretary of Embassy at Paris, formerly H.B.M.'s Chargé d'Affaires, and Secretary of Legation at Yedo. New Edition revised. In 2 vols., with Maps and Plans. Demy 8vo, cloth, price 21s. each

The Ashantee War. A Popular Narrative. By the Special Correspondent of the Daily News. Crown 8vo, cloth, price 6s.

The Russians in Central Asia. A Critical Examination, down to the present time, of the Geography and History of Central Asia. By Baron F. VON HELLWALD. Translated by Lieut.-Col. Theodore Wirgman, LL.B. With Map. Large Post 8vo, cloth, price 12s.

Western India before and during the Mutinies. Pictures drawn from life. By Maj.-Gen. G. LE GRAND JACOB, K.C.S.I., C.B. Second Edition, Crown 8vo, cloth, price 7s. 6d.

The Norman People, and their Existing Descendants in the British Dominions and the United States of America. Demy 8vo, cloth, price 21s.

Echoes of a Famous Year. By HARRIETT PARR. Crown 8vo, cloth, price 8s. 6d.

Persia—Ancient and Modern. By JOHN PIGGOTT, F.S.A., F.R.G.S., Post 8vo, cloth, price 10s. 6d.

Works by NASSAU WILLIAM SENIOR.

Alexis De Tocqueville. Correspondence and Conversation with Nassau W. Senior, from 1833 to 1859. Edited by M.C.M. Simpson. 2 vols. Large Post 8vo, cloth, price 21s.

Journals kept in France and Italy. From 1848 to 1852. With a Sketch of the Revolution of 1848. Edited by his daughter, M. C. M. Simpson. 2 vols, Post 8vo, cloth, price 24s.

History of the English Revolution of 1688. By C. D. YONGE, Regius Professor, Queen's College, Belfast. Crown 8vo, cloth, price 6s.

Rough Notes of a Visit to Belgium, Sedan, and Paris. in September, 1870-71. By JOHN ASHTON. Crown 8vo, cloth, price 3s. 6d.

Field and Forest Rambles of a Naturalist in New Brunswick. With Notes and Observations on the Natural History of Eastern Canada. By A. L. ADAMS, M.A. Illustrated, 8vo, cloth, price 14s.

Eastern Experiences. Illustrated with Maps and Diagrams. By L. BOWRING, C.S.I., Lord Canning's Private Secretary, and for many years Chief Commissioner of Mysore and Coorg. Demy 8vo, cloth, price 16s.

The Inner Life of Syria, Palestine, and the Holy Land. By Mrs. RICHARD BURTON. Second Edition. 2 vols, Demy 8vo, cloth, price 24s.

Round the World in 1870. A Volume of Travels, with Maps. By A. D. CARLISLE, B.A., Trin. Coll., Camb. New and Cheaper Edition. Demy 8vo, cloth, price 6s.

Missionary Enterprise in the East. With special reference to the Syrian Christians of Malabar, and the results of modern Missions. With Four Illustrations. By the Rev. RICHARD COLLINS, M.A. Crown 8vo, cloth, price 6s.

Mountain, Meadow, and Mere. A Series of Outdoor Sketches of Sport, Scenery, Adventures, and Natural History. With Sixteen Illustrations by Bosworth W. Harcourt. By G. CHRISTOPHER DAVIES. Crown 8vo, cloth, price 6s.

The Nile without a Dragoman. By FREDERIC EDEN. Second Edition, Crown 8vo, cloth, price 7s. 6d.

Missionary Life in the Southern Seas. By JAMES HUTTON. With Illustrations. Crown 8vo, cloth, price 7s. 6d.

Letters from China and Japan. By L. D. S. With Illustrated Title-page, Crown 8vo, cloth, price 7s. 6d.

The Truth about Ireland. A Tour of Observation, with Remarks on Irish Public Questions. By JAMES MACAULAY, M.A., M.D., Edin. A New and Cheaper Edition. Crown 8vo, cloth, price 3s. 6d.

Wayside Notes in Scandinavia. Being Notes of Travel in the North of Europe. By MARK ANTONY LOWER, M.A., F.S.A. Crown 8vo, cloth, price 9s.

The Alps of Arabia; or, Travels through Egypt, Sinai, Arabia, and the Holy Land. By WILLIAM CHARLES MAUGHAN. With Map. A New and Cheaper Edition. Demy 8vo, cloth, price 5s.

An Autumn Tour in the United States and Canada. By Lieut.-Col. J. G. MEDLEY, Royal Engineers. Crown 8vo, cloth, price 5s.

A Winter in Morocco. With 4 Illustrations. By AMELIA PERRIER. A New and Cheaper Edition, Crown 8vo, cloth, price 3s. 6d.

Spitzbergen—the Gateway to the Polynia; or, A Voyage to Spitzbergen. With numerous Illustrations by Whymper and others, and Map. By Captain JOHN C. WELLS, R.N. New and Cheaper Edition, 8vo, cloth, price 6s.

The Mishmee Hills: an Account of a Journey made in an Attempt to Penetrate Thibet from Assam, to open New Routes for Commerce. By T. T. COOPER. Second Edition. With Four Illustrations and Map. Demy 8vo, cloth, price 10s. 6d.

'Ilam En Nas. Historical Tales and Anecdotes of the Times of the Early Khalifahs. Translated from the Arabic Originals. Illustrated with Historical and Explanatory Notes. By Mrs. GODFREY CLERK, Author of "The Antipodes and Round the World." Crown 8vo, cloth, price 7s.

Tent Life with English Gipsies in Norway. With Five full-page Engravings and Thirty-one smaller Illustrations by Whymper and others, and Map of the Country showing Routes. By HUBERT SMITH. Third Edition. Revised and Corrected. 8vo, price 21s.

BIOGRAPHY.

JOHN GREY (of Dilston); MEMOIRS. By his Daughter, JOSEPHINE E. BUTLER. New and Cheaper Edition. Crown 8vo, cloth, price 3s. 6d.

The Life of Samuel Lover, R.H.A.; Artistic, Literary, and Musical. With Selections from his Unpublished Papers and Correspondence. By BAYLE BERNARD. 2 Vols. With a Portrait. Post 8vo, cloth, price 21s.

The Earls of Middleton, Lords of Clermont and of Fettercairn, and the Middleton Family. By A. C. BISCOE. Crown 8vo, cloth, price 10s. 6d.

Leonora Christina, Memoirs of, Daughter of Christian IV. of Denmark; Written during her Imprisonment in the Blue Tower of the Royal Palace at Copenhagen, 1663-1685. Translated by F. E. Bunnètt. With an Autotype Portrait of the Princess. A New and Cheaper Edition. Medium 8vo, cloth, price 5s.

Memoir and Letters of Sara Coleridge. Edited by her Daughter. Third Edition, Revised and Corrected. With Index. 2 vols. With 2 Portraits. Crown 8vo, cloth, price 24s.
Cheap Edition. With one Portrait. Crown 8vo, cloth, price 7s. 6d.

Joseph Mazzini: a Memoir. By E. A. V. With two Essays by Mazzini—"Thoughts on Democracy," and "The Duties of Man." Dedicated to the Working Classes by P. H. Taylor, M.P. With Two Portraits. Crown 8vo, cloth, price 3s. 6d.

Mrs. Gilbert, formerly Ann Taylor, Autobiography and other Memorials of. Edited by Josiah Gilbert. New and Revised Edition. In 2 vols. With 2 Steel Portraits and several Wood Engravings. Post 8vo, cloth, price 24s.

The Vicar of Morwenstow: a Memoir of the Rev. R. S. HAWKER. By the Rev. S. BARING-GOULD. New and Revised edition. With Portrait. Post 8vo, cloth, price 10s. 6d.

Autobiography of A. B. Granville, F.R.S., &c. Edited, with a brief account of the concluding years of his life, by his youngest Daughter, PAULINA B. GRANVILLE. 2 vols. With a Portrait. Demy 8vo, cloth, price 32s.

William Augustus, Duke of Cumberland: Being a Sketch of his Military Life and Character, chiefly as exhibited in the General Orders of his Royal Highness, 1745—1747. By ARCHIBALD NEIL CAMPBELL MACLACHLAN, M.A. With Illustrations. Post 8vo, cloth, price 15s.

Characteristics from the Writings of Dr. J. H. Newman. Being Selections, Personal, Historical, Philosophical, and Religious, from his various Works. Arranged with the Author's personal approval. Second Edition. With Portrait. Crown 8vo, cloth, price 6s.

William Godwin: his Friends and Contemporaries. With Portraits and Facsimiles of the handwriting of Godwin and his Wife. By C. KEGAN PAUL. 2 vols. Demy 8vo, cloth, price 28s.

The late Rev. F. W. Robertson, M.A., Life and Letters of. Edited by STOPFORD BROOKE, M.A.
  I. In 2 vols., uniform with the Sermons. Steel Portrait. 7s. 6d.
  II. Library Edition. 8vo. Two Steel Portraits. 12s.
  III. A Popular Edition, in 1 vol. 8vo. 6s.

Life and Letters of Rowland Williams, D.D. With Selections from his Note-books. Edited by Mrs. ROWLAND WILLIAMS. With a Photographic Portrait. 2 vols. Large post 8vo, cloth, price 24s.

Shelley Memorials from Authentic Sources. With (now first printed) an Essay on Christianity by PERCY BYSSHE SHELLEY. With Portrait. Third Edition. Crown 8vo, cloth, price 5s.

Memoirs of Gen. W. T. Sherman, Commander of the Federal Forces in the American Civil War. By Himself. With Map. 2 vols. Demy 8vo, cloth, price 24s. *Copyright English Edition.*

Cabinet Portraits. Biographical Sketches of Statesmen of the Day. By T. WEMYSS REID. Crown 8vo, cloth, price 7s. 6d.

THEOLOGY.

**SCOTCH COMMUNION SUNDAY**, to which are added Certain Discourses from a University City. By A. K. H. B., the Author of "The Recreations of a Country Parson. Second Edition. Crown 8vo, cloth, price 5s.

Abraham: his Life, Times, and Travels, as told by a Contemporary 3,800 years ago. With Map. By the Rev. R. ALLEN, M.A. Post 8vo, cloth, price 10s. 6d.

Works by the Rev. CHARLES ANDERSON, M.A.

Church Thought and Church Work. Edited by. Second Edition, Demy 8vo, cloth, price 7s. 6d.

Containing Articles by the Revs.—

J. M. Capes,
Professor Cheetham,
J. Ll. Davis,
Harry Jones,

Brooke Lambert,
A. J. Ross,
The Editor,
And others.

Words and Works in a London Parish. Edited by. Second Edition, Demy 8vo, cloth, price 6s.

The Curate of Shyre. Second Edition. 8vo, cloth, price 7s. 6d.

New Readings of Old Parables. Demy 8vo, cloth, price 4s. 6d.

The Eternal Life. Sermons by the Rev. JAS. NOBLE BENNIE, M.A. Crown 8vo, cloth, price 6s.

Works by the Rev. J. BALDWIN BROWN, B.A.

The Higher Life. Its Reality, Experience, and Destiny. Fourth Edition, Crown 8vo, cloth, price 7s. 6d.

The Doctrine of Annihilation in the Light of the Gospel of Love. Five Discourses. Second Edition Crown 8vo, cloth, price 2s. 6d.

Until the Day Dawn. Four Advent Lectures By the Rev. MARMADUKE E. BROWNE. Crown 8vo, cloth, price 2s. 6d.

Works by W. G. BROOKE, M.A., Barrister-at-Law.

The Public Worship Regulation Act. With a Classified Statement of its Provisions, Notes, and Index. Third Edition, revised and corrected, Crown 8vo, cloth, price 3s. 6d.

Six Privy Council Judgments—1850-1872. Annotated by. Third Edition, Crown 8vo, cloth, price 9s.

Works by the Rev. STOPFORD A. BROOKE, M.A.,
Chaplain-in-Ordinary to H.M. the Queen.

Theology in the English Poets. Cowper, Coleridge, Wordsworth, and Burns. Second Edition, post 8vo, cloth, price 9s.

Freedom in the Church of England. Six Sermons suggested by the Voysey judgment. Second Edition, Crown 8vo, cloth, price 3s. 6d.

Christ in Modern Life. Sermons. Eighth Edition, Crown 8vo, cloth, price 7s. 6d.

Sermons. First Series, Eighth Edition, Crown 8vo, cloth, price 6s.

Sermons. Second Series, Third Edition, Crown 8vo, cloth, price 7s.

The Life and Work of Frederick Denison Maurice. A Memorial Sermon. Crown 8vo, sewed, price 1s.

The Realm of Truth. By Miss E. T. CARNE. Crown 8vo, cloth, price 5s. 6d.

The New Testament, translated from the latest Greek Text of Tischendorf. By SAMUEL DAVIDSON, D.D., LL.D. A new and thoroughly revised Edition. Post 8vo, cloth, price 10s. 6d.

Why am I a Christian? By Viscount STRATFORD DE REDCLIFFE, P.C., K.G., G.C.B. Fifth Edition, Crown 8vo, cloth, price 3s.

Works by the Rev. G. S. DREW, M.A., Vicar of Trinity, Lambeth.

The Son of Man, His Life and Ministry. Crown 8vo, cloth, price 7s. 6d.

Scripture Lands in Connection with their History. Second Edition, 8vo, cloth, price 10s. 6d.

Nazareth: Its Life and Lessons. Third Edition, Crown 8vo, cloth, price 5s.

The Divine Kingdom on Earth as it is in Heaven. Demy 8vo, cloth, price 10s. 6d.

An Essay on the Rule of Faith and Creed of Athanasius. By an ENGLISH CLERGYMAN. 8vo, sewed, price 1s.

A Book of Common Prayer and Worship for Household use, compiled from the Holy Scriptures. By MARK EVANS. Foolscap 8vo, cloth, price 2s. 6d.

Studies of the Divine Master. By the Rev. T. GRIFFITH, A.M., Prebendary of St. Paul's. Demy 8vo, cloth, price 12s.

Rugby School Sermons. By HENRY HAYMAN, D.D., late Head Master of Rugby School. With an Introductory Essay on the Indwelling of the Holy Spirit. Crown 8vo, cloth, price 7s. 6d.

Works by the Rev. H. R. HAWEIS, M.A.

Speech in Season. Third Edition. Crown 8vo, cloth, price 9s.

Thoughts for the Times. Ninth Edition. Crown 8vo, cloth, price 7s. 6d.

Unsectarian Family Prayers, for Morning and Evening for a Week, with short selected passages from the Bible. Square Crown 8vo, cloth, price 3s. 6d.

The Privilege of Peter, Legally and Historically Examined, and the claims of the Roman Church compared with the Scriptures, the Councils, and the Testimony of the Popes themselves. By the Rev. R. C. JENKINS, M.A., Rector of Lyminge, and Honorary Canon of Canterbury. Foolscap 8vo, cloth, price 3s. 6d.

The Gospel its own Witness. By the Rev. STANLEY LEATHES. Crown 8vo, cloth, price 5s.

John Knox and the Church of England: His Work in her Pulpit and his Influence upon her Liturgy, Articles, and Parties. By PETER LORIMER, D.D. Demy 8vo, cloth, price 12s.

Essays on Religion and Literature. By various Writers. Edited by His Eminence Cardinal MANNING. Demy 8vo, cloth, price 10s. 6d.

CONTENTS.

The Philosophy of Christianity.
Mystic Elements of Religion.
Controversy with the Agnostics.
A Reasoning Thought.
Darwinism brought to Book.

Mr. Mill on Liberty of the Press
Christianity in relation to Society.
The Religious Condition of Germany.
The Philosophy of Bacon.

Catholic Laymen and Scholastic Philosophy.

Sermonettes: on Synonymous Texts, taken from the Bible and Book of Common Prayer, for the Study, Family Reading, and Private Devotion. By the Rev. THOMAS MOORE, Vicar of Christ Church, Chesham. Small Crown 8vo, cloth, price 4s. 6d.

Christ and His Church. A Course of Lent Lectures, By the Rev. DANIEL MOORE, M.A., Author of "The Age and the Gospel," &c. Crown 8vo, cloth, price 3s. 6d.

The Paraclete: An Essay on the Personality and Ministry of the Holy Ghost, with some reference to current discussions. By JOSEPH PARKER, D.D. Second Edition. Demy 8vo, cloth, price 12s.

Unfoldings of Christian Hope: An Essay showing that the Doctrine contained in the Damnatory Clauses of the Creed commonly called Athanasian is unscriptural. By PRESBYTER. Small Crown 8vo, cloth, price 4s. 6d.

Works by the late Rev. F. W. ROBERTSON, M.A.

Sermons. New and Cheaper Editions.
> First Series.—Small Crown 8vo, cloth, price 3s. 6d.
> Second Series.—Small Crown 8vo, cloth, price 3s. 6d.
> Third Series.—Small Crown 8vo, cloth, price 3s. 6d.
> Fourth Series.—Small Crown 8vo, cloth, price 3s. 6d.

Expository Lectures on St. Paul's Epistle to the Corinthians. Small Crown 8vo, cloth, price 5s.

Lectures and Addresses, with other Literary Remains. A New Edition. Crown 8vo, cloth, price 5s.

> The above Works can also be had bound in half Morocco.

An Analysis of Mr. Tennyson's "In Memoriam." Dedicated, by Permission, to the Poet-Laureate. Foolscap 8vo, cloth, price 2s.

The Education of the Human Race. Translated from the German of Gotthold Ephraim Lessing. Foolscap 8vo, cloth, price 2s. 6d.

Studies in Modern Problems. By various Writers. Edited by the Rev. ORBY SHIPLEY, M.A. 2 vols. Crown 8vo, cloth, price 5s. each.

Home Words for Wanderers. A Volume of Sermons. By the Rev. A. S. THOMPSON, British Chaplain at St. Petersburg, Crown 8vo, cloth, price 6s.

Every Day a Portion. Adapted from the Bible and the Prayer Book, for the Private Devotions of those living in Widowhood. Collected and Edited by Lady MARY VYNER. Square Crown 8vo, cloth, price 5s.

WORKS by the Rev. C. J. VAUGHAN, D.D.

Words of Hope from the Pulpit of the Temple Church.
Third Edition. Crown 8vo, cloth, price 5s.

The Solidity of True Religion, and other Sermons.
Crown 8vo, cloth, price 3s. 6d.

Forget Thine Own People. An Appeal for Missions.
Crown 8vo, cloth, price 3s. 6d.

The Young Life Equipping Itself for God's Service.
Being Four Sermons Preached before the University of Cambridge, in November, 1872. Fourth Edition. Crown 8vo, cloth, price 3s. 6d.

Catholicism and the Vatican. With a Narrative of the Old Catholic Congress at Munich. By J. LOWRY WHITTLE, A.M., Trin. Coll., Dublin. Second Edition. Crown 8vo, cloth, price 4s. 6d.

The Church and the Empires. Historical Periods. By HENRY W. WILBERFORCE. Preceded by a Memoir of the Author by John Henry Newman, D.D., of the Oratory. With Portrait. Post 8vo, cloth, price 10s. 6d.

Works by the Rev. D. WRIGHT, of Stoke Bishop, Bristol.

Man and Animals. A Sermon. Crown 8vo, stitched in wrapper, price 1s.

Waiting for the Light, and other Sermons. Crown 8vo, cloth, price 6s.

SCIENCE.

THE PRINCIPLES of MENTAL PHYSIOLOGY. By W. B. CARPENTER, LL.D., M.D., F.R.S., &c. Illustrated. Large post 8vo, cloth, price 12s.

The Scientific Societies of London. By BERNARD H. BECKER. Crown 8vo, cloth, price 5s.

Works by JAMES HINTON, late Aural Surgeon to Guy's Hospital.

The Place of the Physician. Being the Introductory Lecture at Guy's Hospital, 1873-74. To which is added Essays on the Law of Human Life, and on the Relation between Organic and Inorganic Worlds. Second Edition. Crown 8vo, cloth, price 3s. 6d.

Physiology for Practical Use. By various Writers. Second Edition. Illustrated. 2 vols., Crown 8vo, cloth, price 12s. 6d.

An Atlas of Diseases of the Membrana Tympani. With Descriptive Text. Post 8vo, price £6 6s.

The Questions of Aural Surgery. Illustrated. 2 vols., Post 8vo, cloth, price 12s. 6d.

Works by RICHARD A. PROCTOR.

Our Place among Infinities. A Series of Essays contrasting our little abode in space and time with the Infinities around us. To which are added Essays on "Astrology," and "The Jewish Sabbath." Second Edition. Crown 8vo, cloth, price 6s.

The Expanse of Heaven. A Series of Essays on the Wonders of the Firmament. With a Frontispiece. Second Edition. Crown 8vo, cloth, price 6s.

Works by Professor TH. RIBOT.

Contemporary English Psychology. Second Edition. Revised. Large post 8vo, cloth, price 9s.

Heredity: A Psychological Study on its Phenomena, its Laws, its Causes, and its Consequences. Large Crown 8vo, cloth, price 9s.

The Physics and Philosophy of the Senses; or, The Mental and the Physical in their Mutual Relation. Illustrated. By R. S. WYLD, F.R.S.E. Demy 8vo, cloth, price 16s.

Sensation and Intuition. By JAMES SULLY. Demy 8vo, cloth, price 10s. 6d.

THE INTERNATIONAL SCIENTIFIC SERIES.

1. **The Forms of Water in Clouds and Rivers, Ice and Glaciers.** By J. TYNDALL, LL.D., F.R.S. With 14 Illustrations. Sixth Edition. Crown 8vo, cloth, price 5s.

2. **Physics and Politics; or, Thoughts on the Application** of the Principles of "Natural Selection" and "Inheritance" to Political Society. By WALTER BAGEHOT. Third Edition. Crown 8vo, cloth, price 4s.

3. **Foods.** By EDWARD SMITH, M.D., LL.B., F.R.S. Profusely Illustrated. Fourth Edition. Crown 8vo, cloth, price 5s.

4. **Mind and Body: the Theories of their Relation.** By ALEXANDER BAIN, LL.D. With 4 Illustrations. Fifth Edition. Crown 8vo, cloth, price 4s.

5. **The Study of Sociology.** By HERBERT SPENCER. Fifth Edition. Crown 8vo, cloth, price 5s.

6. **On the Conservation of Energy.** By BALFOUR STEWART, M.D., LL.D., F.R.S. With 14 Engravings. Third Edition. Crown 8vo, cloth, price 5s.

7. **Animal Locomotion; or, Walking, Swimming, and Flying.** By J. B. PETTIGREW, M.D., F.R.S. With 119 Illustrations. Second Edition. Crown 8vo, cloth, price 5s.

8. **Responsibility in Mental Disease.** By H. MAUDSLEY, M.D. Second Edition. Crown 8vo, cloth, price 5s.

9. **The New Chemistry.** By Professor J. P. COOKE, of the Harvard University. With 31 Illustrations. Third Edition. Crown 8vo, cloth, price 5s.

10. **The Science of Law.** By Professor SHELDON AMOS. Second Edition. Crown 8vo, cloth, price 5s.

11. **Animal Mechanism.** A Treatise on Terrestrial and Aërial Locomotion. By Professor E. J. MAREY. With 117 Illustrations. Second Edition. Crown 8vo, cloth, price 5s.

12. **The Doctrine of Descent and Darwinism.** By Professor OSCAR SCHMIDT (Strasburg University). With 26 Illustrations. Third Edition. Crown 8vo, cloth, price 5s.

13. **The History of the Conflict between Religion and Science.** By Professor J. W. DRAPER. Seventh Edition. Crown 8vo, cloth, price 5s.

14. **Fungi: their Nature, Influences, Uses, &c.** By M. C. COOKE, M.A., LL.D. Edited by the Rev. M. J. Berkeley, M.A., F.L.S. With numerous Illustrations. Second Edition. Crown 8vo, cloth, price 5s.

15. **The Chemical Effects of Light and Photography.** By Dr. HERMANN VOGEL (Polytechnic Academy of Berlin). Translation thoroughly revised. With 100 Illustrations. Third Edition. Crown 8vo, cloth, price 5s.

16. **The Life and Growth of Language.** By WILLIAM DWIGHT WHITNEY, Professor of Sanskrit and Comparative Philology in Yale College, New Haven. Second Edition. Crown 8vo, cloth, price 5s.

17. **Money and the Mechanism of Exchange.** By Professor W. STANLEY JEVONS. Second Edition. Crown 8vo, cloth, price 5s.

18. **The Nature of Light: With a General Account of Physical Optics.** By Dr. EUGENE LOMMEL, Professor of Physics in the University of Erlangen. With 188 Illustrations, and a Table of Spectra in Chromolithography. Second Edition. Crown 8vo, cloth, price 5s.

19. **Animal Parasites & Messmates.** By M. VAN BENEDEN, Professor of the University of Louvain, Correspondent of the Institute of France. With 83 Illustrations. Second Edition. Crown 8vo, cloth, price 5s.

20. **Fermentation.** By Professor SCHUTZENBERGER, Director of the Chemical Laboratory at the Sorbonne. Second Edition. Crown 8vo, cloth, 5s.

21. **The Five Senses of Man.** By Professor BERNSTEIN, of the University of Halle. With 91 Illustrations. Crown 8vo, cloth, price 5s.

MISCELLANEOUS.

Works by WALTER BAGEHOT.

LOMBARD STREET. A Description of the Money Market. Sixth Edition. Crown 8vo, cloth, price 7s. 6d.

The English Constitution. A New Edition, Revised and corrected. Crown 8vo, cloth, price 7s. 6d.

Physics and Politics; or, Thoughts on the Application of the Principles of "Natural Selection" and "Inheritance" to Political Society. Third Edition. Crown 8vo, cloth, price 4s.

Volume II. of the International Scientific Series.

About My Father's Business. Work amidst the Sick, the Sad, and the Sorrowing. By THOMAS ARCHER. Crown 8vo, cloth, price 5s.

Studies in English. For the Use of Modern Schools. By H. C. Bowen, English Master Middle-Class City School, Cowper-street. Small Crown 8vo, cloth, price 1s. 6d.

Works by JOHN CROUMBIE BROWN, LL.D., &c.

Reboisement in France; or, Records of the Replanting of the Alps, the Cevennes, and the Pyrenees with Trees, Herbage, and Bush, with a view to arresting and preventing the destructive consequences and effects of Torrents. Demy 8vo, cloth, price 12s. 6d.

The Hydrology of Southern Africa. Demy 8vo, cloth, price 10s. 6d.

Republican Superstitions. Illustrated by the Political History of the United States. Including a correspondence with M. Louis Blanc. By MONCURE D. CONWAY. Crown 8vo, cloth, price 5s.

Works by Edward Clodd, F.R.A.S.

The Childhood of the World: a Simple Account of Man in Early Times. New Edition. Crown 8vo, cloth, price 3s.
A Special Edition for Schools. Limp cloth, price 1s.

The Childhood of Religions. Including a Simple Account of the Birth and Growth of Myths and Legends. Crown 8vo, cloth, price 5s.

Shakspere: a Critical Study of his Mind and Art. By Edward Dowden, LL.D. Second Edition. Post 8vo, cloth, price 12s.

The Better Self. Essays for Home Life. By J. Hain Friswell. Crown 8vo, cloth, price 6s.

CONTENTS.

Beginning at Home.	Domestic Economy.
The Girls at Home.	On Keeping People Down.
The Wife's Mother.	Likes and Dislikes.
Pride in the Family.	On Falling Out.
Discontent and Grumbling.	Peace.

Myths and Songs of the South Pacific. With a Preface by F. Max Müller, M.A., Professor of Comparative Philology at Oxford. By the Rev. W. W. Gill. Post 8vo, cloth, price 9s.

Memorials of Millbank, and Chapters in Prison History. By Captain Arthur Griffiths. With Illustrations. 2 vol. Post 8vo, cloth, price 21s.

The Other World; or, Glimpses of the Supernatural. Being Facts, Records, and Traditions, relating to Dreams, Omens, Miraculous Occurrences, Apparitions, Wraiths, Warnings, Second-sight, Necromancy, Witchcraft, &c. By Rev. Frederick George Lee, D.C.L. A New Edition. 2 vols., Crown 8vo, cloth, price 15s.

Currency and Banking. By Professor Bonamy Price, Professor of Political Economy at Oxford. Crown 8vo, cloth, price 6s.

PORTRAITS OF AUTHORS.

Steel Engravings, Large India Proofs, Suitable for framing
price 2s. 6d. each.

Dr. W. C. Bennett.

Robert Buchanan.

Sara Coleridge (Ætat. 17).

Sara Coleridge (in after years).

Mrs. Ann Gilbert.

Samuel Lover.

John Henry Newman.

F. W. Robertson.

Percy B. Shelley.

Alfred Tennyson.

H. W. Wilberforce.

UNWIN BROTHERS, PRINTERS, LONDON AND CHILWORTH.

www.ingramcontent.com/pod-product-compliance
Lightning Source LLC
Chambersburg PA
CBHW021804230426
43669CB00008B/632